FRESHW
FiSH
OF BRITAIN AND EUROPE

WITHDRAWN

FRESHWATER FISHES
OF BRITAIN AND EUROPE

ALWYNE WHEELER

Illustrated by
Norman Weever, Denys Ovenden
and Alan Male

RAINBOW
· BOOKS ·

This edition published in 1992 by Rainbow Books,
Elsley House, 24–30 Great Titchfield Street, London W1P 7AD.

Originally published in 1983 as a Kingfisher Guide to Freshwater Fishes.

ISBN 1 871745 88 8

Printed and bound in Italy

CONTENTS

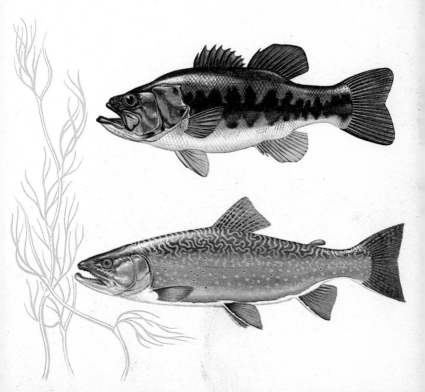

INTRODUCTION

Fishes are the most abundant group of vertebrate animals in existence. It is estimated that there are about 20,000 known kinds of fish, more than all the other vertebrates – mammals, birds, reptiles and amphibians – added together. With such a very large number, it is not surprising that there is a huge variation in body form and size among fishes; sizes ranging from the whale shark of the tropical seas, *Rhincodon typus*, which reaches a length of 18 metres, to the Philippine Islands goby, *Pandaka pygmaea*, which never grows longer than 11 millimetres. In European fresh waters, lengths are less extreme but are nevertheless impressive, with the beluga, *Huso huso*, reaching 5 metres and the tiny Spanish toothcarp, *Aphanius iberus*, only 5 centimetres.

All these fishes have several features in common. They use gills to extract oxygen from the water, their blood is circulated around the body by means of a chambered heart, and they have a backbone. This consists of a series of separate vertebrae joined together by tough ligaments, which gives a degree of flexibility without losing the strength of a continuous rod. They also have a skull or cranium which contains and protects the brain and the roots of the major nerves. The brain is well-developed, with distinct regions concerned with separate sensory functions, such as sight and smell. Fishes all have fins, although in some species they are better developed than in others, depending on the animal's life style. In most species, they play an important role in swimming.

These fundamental characteristics set fishes apart from other animals which live in the water. Whales and porpoises, which are grouped with the vertebrates, are not fishes because they breathe air with their lungs. Crayfish, cuttlefish and shellfish generally are not fishes because they lack a backbone, a skull, fins, and a chambered heart, and they belong to the animal group known as invertebrates.

The variety and the very great number of fishes in the world is not perhaps surprising, considering the space available to them. Something like seven-tenths of the globe is covered by the oceans, and a further one-hundredth is covered by fresh water. This reflects the proportions of marine and freshwater fishes: on a world basis there are estimated to be about 13,000 sea fish and 7,000 freshwater known at present. Fresh waters offer much less living space than the sea; they are never so deep, and they tend to have fewer niches which can be exploited. Yet Europe's freshwater fishes have developed an admirable opportunism which enables them to live in most of its rivers and lakes, though the variety of species and the number of individuals are fewer in the more hostile environments of high mountains and Arctic conditions.

Brook charr are North American relatives of the trout, introduced to Europe for their angling potential; they are also good to eat.

The Classification of Fishes

There are three major groups of living fishes: the lampreys and their relatives, sharks and rays, and bony fishes. The groups are not of equal size – on a world basis there are about 38 lampreys, about 630 sharks and relatives, and over 19,000 bony fishes – nor are they of equal relationship.

The lampreys and hagfishes belong to the Superclass Agnatha – the jawless fishes. They have no jaws, no pectoral or pelvic fins, and their other fins are low fleshy folds with very fine cartilaginous supports. They have no real tail fin and their skeletons are composed entirely of cartilage.

Sharks and rays and bony fishes belong to the Superclass Gnathostomata – fishes with jaws – but the sharks and rays are subdivided as the Class Chondrichthyes (the cartilaginous fishes). Their skeletons are made up entirely of cartilage and they have well-developed fins, strengthened with thin cartilaginous rays. Their jaws are well-equipped with teeth, which are replaced constantly and in series. They have no swimbladder.

The bony fishes, which dominate the fresh waters of Europe, as they do worldwide, belong to the Class Osteichthyes. Much of their skeleton is composed of bone. They have well-developed fins with strong bony fin rays. Their jaws have variable numbers of teeth and most have a swimbladder. They are numerous in the sea as well as in fresh water.

Within these classes, fish species, like all animals, are arranged in orders, families and genera. The basic category is the species – which is given a scientific name either in Latin or in latinized form. Thus the first species in the book, the sea lamprey, bears the name *Petromyzon marinus*, the first word being the genus name and the second being the specific name. They are derived from the Greek words *petros*, a stone, *muzo*, to suck, and the Latin adjective for *mare*, sea. So the name means a stone sucker that travels to the sea – a name quite descriptive of its life history and habits.

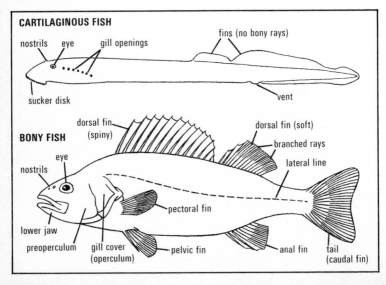

THE CLASSIFICATION OF EUROPEAN FRESHWATER FISHES

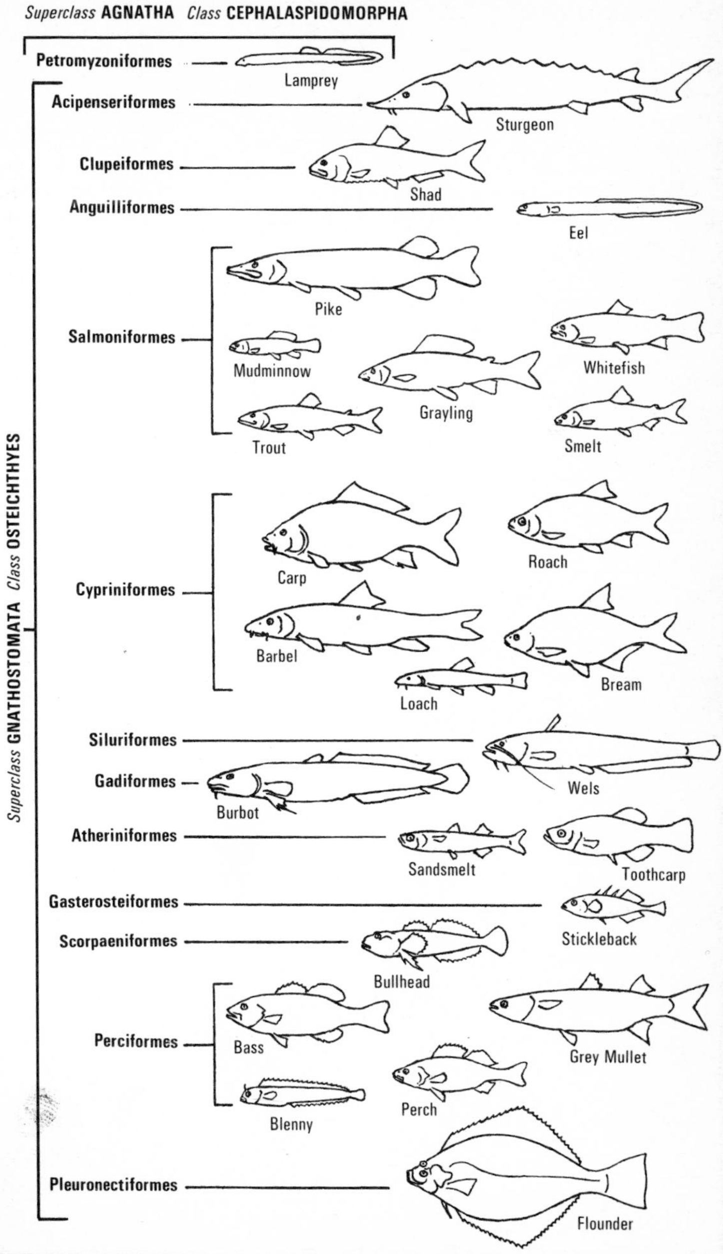

Superclass **AGNATHA** *Class* **CEPHALASPIDOMORPHA**

Petromyzoniformes — Lamprey

Acipenseriformes — Sturgeon

Clupeiformes — Shad

Anguilliformes — Eel

Salmoniformes — Pike, Mudminnow, Grayling, Trout, Whitefish, Smelt

Cypriniformes — Carp, Roach, Barbel, Loach, Bream

Siluriformes — Wels

Gadiformes — Burbot

Atheriniformes — Sandsmelt, Toothcarp

Gasterosteiformes — Stickleback

Scorpaeniformes — Bullhead

Perciformes — Bass, Blenny, Perch, Grey Mullet

Pleuronectiformes — Flounder

Superclass **GNATHOSTOMATA** *Class* **OSTEICHTHYES**

The Distribution of Fishes in Europe

Freshwater fishes are not evenly distributed over the whole of Europe. There are many more species in the east and south-east of Europe than there are at its western and northern extremities. This is not due to lack of suitable habitats, or to the harsh winters of the north, but is a reflection of the geological history of Europe and the speed with which groups or species spread into suitable habitats.

Fishes found in rivers and lakes are divided into three basic types according to their ability to tolerate salt water. Most freshwater fishes, including members of the carp family, loaches, catfishes, the perch family and the pike, cannot live in water which is one third as salt as the sea. They are called primary freshwater fishes. A second group, including some members of the salmon family, toothcarps and sticklebacks, can survive in the sea for at least a short while. They are the secondary freshwater fishes. The third group, which can come and go between the sea and rivers without inconvenience, includes the salmon, the sturgeon, some lampreys and the eel.

The most important factor affecting Europe's fishes was the series of ice ages which covered the land in varying degrees during the Pleistocene period. The last of these occurred some 50,000 years ago. During these glacial episodes, ice from the Arctic advanced to cover much of northern Europe, and it also increased in mountainous regions to the south, such as the Pyrenees and the Alps, so that the whole continent became much colder. Many rivers and all upland lakes were frozen for most of the year. The level of the sea also fell, so in places the coastline was very different from that of today. The effect of these subarctic conditions on the fishes was severe. Primary freshwater fishes were trapped in the frozen rivers and eventually wiped out, while the secondary fishes migrated southwards through the sea. This meant that there were no freshwater fishes in northern Europe following the biggest of the ice ages, while those to the south were trapped, but survived in refuges. Most of the Iberian, Italian and Balkan peninsulas were refuges, as was the River Rhône in southern France, and the fishes living in these regions are in some cases descendants of the pre-glacial fauna. These areas also have numerous endemic species – that is species which are found nowhere else. The most important glacial refuge, however, was the River Danube, which flows to the south and east, and which offered a shelter to many primary species.

Following the retreat of the ice, the climate became warmer and the rivers of northern Europe were habitable once more. The secondary freshwater fishes, like the trout and stickleback, moved northwards colonizing rivers as the ice retreated. Sometimes they left populations cut off in their refuges to the south, which is the reason that small stocks of trout and sticklebacks still occur in the rivers of western North Africa. The primary freshwater fishes could not recolonize through the sea, but they gradually spread into northern Europe from their refuges as floods and land movements temporarily joined river systems together. Thus, the freshwater fishes moved westwards and northwards from the Danube refuge, some moving faster and further than others, spreading through Germany, southern Scandinavia, France, and the Low Countries. Until about 13,000 years ago, England was still joined to the continent of Europe and some species were able to pass through the swampy peatlands that occupied the bed of the present North Sea to reach English rivers, and thus spread from there. But Ireland was already an island before this happened, so no primary freshwater fishes occur there naturally.

Other fishes, like the whitefishes, which are well able to withstand cold, spread through Europe in the ice lakes that formed soon after the ice melted. However, as these lakes dried up with the retreat of the ice, populations of whitefishes were isolated in mountain lakes in the Alps, and in the British Isles. They are also present in many lakes in Scandinavia.

As the human race became dominant in Europe, many species of fishes were redistributed. The Danubian wels, the zander and the carp, for example, are now found in many parts of Europe, and several freshwater species have been introduced to Ireland. Many exotic species, like the American rainbow trout and the freshwater basses, have also been introduced and are now widespread in Europe. Human interference has both enriched and obscured the natural distribution of Europe's freshwater fish fauna.

THE MAJOR RIVERS OF EUROPE

Freshwater Habitats

The greatest variety of freshwater fishes live in rivers. This is a reflection of the differing habitats that a river offers – many more than a still water, whether it is a mountain or a lowland lake. For a river is not homogenous from its source to its mouth but changes with the type of terrain through which it flows.

At its source, always in hilly country and often in the mountains, a river is narrow; the slope of its bed is steep and its current fast. It often flows over small waterfalls – sometimes only a boulder a metre high, sometimes a fall of several metres. This causes the water to be well oxygenated, because it is constantly mixed with air at the falls. The water is cold, which means it can absorb more dissolved oxygen, and clear, because there is little mud in the river bed and few water plants can establish themselves. The only fishes found in this habitat are small trout, bullhead and the occasional minnow.

Downstream the bed of the river is less steep, but the water still flows fast. It has deeper pools and shallows, and is cool and clear in summer. Plants root in the mud at the river bank in sheltered spots. This area is inhabited by grayling, minnows and trout, as well as salmon, which breed here. In the Danube system, this is also the habitat of the huchen and the nase.

Below this, the slope of the river becomes more gentle and the current is moderate. The water is fairly warm, and usually rather turbid due to plant plankton and mud in suspension. Dissolved oxygen is moderately high at the surface, and below weirs, but lower near the river bed. This is known as the barbel zone, but chub, dace and roach also occur, preyed on by pike and, when young, by perch. Salmon and eels are common. In the Danube, nases, zander and some of the perch relatives are found.

Further downstream, where the slope becomes very gentle, this region merges into the bream zone. Here the bottom is sand and gravel mixed with mud, and the current is slow. The water is warm in summer, and always turbid. Dissolved oxygen is moderately high at the surface, lower near the river bed. In addition to the bream, roach, carp, tench, pike, wels, burbot and various bream relatives are found. At its lower end, this region – often influenced by tides, although the water is not salt – gives way to the estuary.

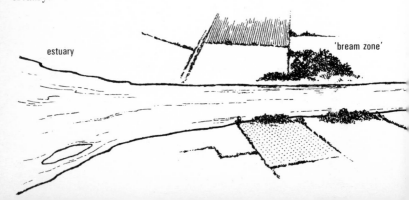

The estuary, which becomes increasingly salt and muddy, is an important habitat for fishes like smelt, shads and flounder, while the sturgeon, salmon and eel pass through it on their spawning and feeding migrations. With its warm water, rich feeding grounds and protective shallows, the estuary is also an important nursery area for many inshore marine fishes.

Lowland lakes have most of the characteristic physical features of the bream zone, and the fishes typical of this zone thrive in them. In Europe, many such lakes are man-made gravel pits, reservoirs or ornamental waters. In mountainous areas, however, the lakes are very different. Usually stony-bottomed, with mud in the deeper areas, they are cold and clear. Plant and animal life are sparse. Trout, minnows and bullhead are found there, as well as charr and whitefishes. In much of Europe, however, this habitat has been adversely affected by the discharge of effluents, by agriculture, by using the lakes for water storage, and by the introduction of other species of fish.

THE RIVER FROM SOURCE TO SEA

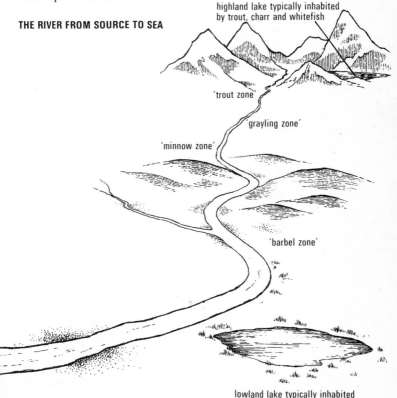

highland lake typically inhabited by trout, charr and whitefish

'trout zone'

grayling zone'

'minnow zone'

'barbel zone'

lowland lake typically inhabited by carp family fish, perch and pike

The Anatomy of the Fish

Fishes are covered by a relatively tough skin, composed of several layers. The extreme outer covering, the epidermis, is thin and virtually transparent; it overlies the scales covering both sides of their free edge. It contains large cells which give off the slippery mucus so characteristic of fishes, and their fishy odour. This mucus is mildly antiseptic and resists infection; it also helps the fish to slip through the water. Within the layer of the skin lie the scales, arranged to overlap one another like tiles on a roof. They give protection to the muscles which lie beneath the skin but, because they are only fastened at their front end, do not hinder the fish as it swims. As it flexes its body, the scales simply slide over one another.

The number of scales is unchanging in a fish from soon after hatching. As the fish grows, each scale grows larger on its underside and edge. There are big differences in growth rate between winter and summer, which are shown as differently spaced growth rings on the scales. By counting these rings, it is possible to tell how old a fish is.

Beneath the scales lie deeper layers of skin in which the colour cells are formed. These are basically of three kinds: black, red and orange, and yellow, and each cell can expand and contract to obtain a range of shades which match the fish's background. This works in response to information about its surroundings which the fish receives through the eyes. A fourth kind of cell contains the silvery crystals which make so many fishes silvery in colour, but these are not capable of expansion.

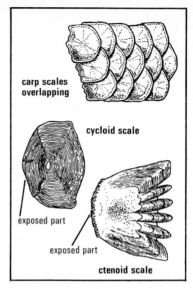

carp scales overlapping

cycloid scale

exposed part

exposed part

ctenoid scale

The arrangement of scales on the fish's body provides a tough protective covering. Scales are either cycloid (e.g. carp family) or ctenoid (e.g. perch family).

Muscles

Although all the spines and rays of the fins have muscles attached to them which raise or lower the fin element, the major musculature of the fish is in its body. These muscles, each of which is attached to a vertebra in the backbone, provide the power for the fish when it swims, and pull or relax so that the tail is swung from side to side. Beneath the skin, the muscles can be seen lying in zig-zag shaped blocks. Most of the muscle is pale-coloured, like the 'sprinting muscle' used when the fish is attacking or trying to escape, but along the side of the body towards the tail there is a stripe of darker muscle which is used for cruising, allowing the fish to swim day after day without fatigue.

Respiration

Like all animals, fishes depend on oxygen to survive. Air-breathing animals live in an atmosphere containing about 20 per cent oxygen, but fishes have to get their oxygen from the water, which contains only 1–5 per cent oxygen. This means that their oxygen-collecting system has to be very efficient.

A fish's blood contains the same oxygen-carrying red blood cells found in humans, but they are much smaller. However, they still contain the same iron compound haemaglobin which carries the dissolved oxygen around the body in the arteries.

The gills are the essential organ for recharging the blood with oxygen. Blood is pumped directly to the gills through arteries which are ever more finely branched. Within the feathery gill, the red blood cells are separated by only a thin membrane from oxygen-rich water sucked in through the mouth. In this way, oxygen is taken up by the blood, replacing carbon dioxide and other waste products.

A 'breathing' fish can be seen opening its mouth to take in water. The mouth is then closed, sealed off by interior flaps, the floor of the throat is raised and the water is forced over and through the gills which lie on the outside of the gill arch, and then out through the gill opening. As most fish have the same body temperature as that of the water, their oxygen requirements vary with its temperature. In winter they need less, while in summer, when the water holds less oxygen anyway, they have to gulp water more frequently. If the oxygen level falls too low, they may gulp at the surface, where the surface water is better oxygenated.

The gills of the fish absorb oxygen from the water and get rid of carbon dioxide from the blood. Water is taken in through the mouth, which expands, and then expelled through the gill openings.

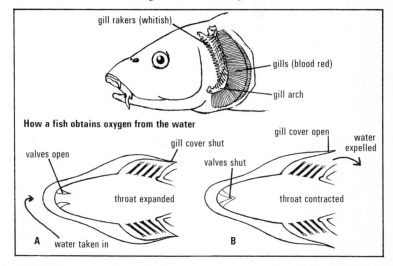

gill rakers (whitish)

gills (blood red)

gill arch

How a fish obtains oxygen from the water

valves open

gill cover shut

throat expanded

A water taken in

gill cover open

water expelled

valves shut

throat contracted

B

The Senses

It is often thought that fishes are short-sighted and cannot see well – probably because of their bulging eyes. In fact, they can see as well as their habitat allows; and they are mostly long-sighted. In the forward field, their vision is acute, so that they can see prey when it is close up; but at the sides and to the rear, their eyes are well adapted to detect movement – enabling them to keep their place in a school or to detect a moving predator. Much of the water's surface above them will, however, be a silvery mirror, clear on still days and reflecting the bottom, but usually ruffled by the wind. In the centre of their visual field, fish can see clearly through the surface layer – and more widely than might be supposed due to refraction at the surface. Anglers standing on the bank are often clearly seen. Many fishes can also see in colour.

While food items can be seen at a distance, fishes need to touch the object before they can taste it. Barbels around the mouth are particularly well supplied with taste organs, which are widely distributed on the lips and chin, so a fish does not have to take an angler's bait into its mouth to find out if it is edible.

The sense of smell is also acute in most fishes. Some, like the burbot and the eel, which feed mainly at night, have notably large nasal organs. All European freshwater fishes have two nostrils on each side of the head, each with an entrance and an exit. Thus the fish can circulate a continuous stream of water over the sensitive rosette of the nasal organ and constantly sample the odour particles in the water.

Members of the carp family have a particularly well-developed sense of smell for the substance released by an injured individual of their own species. This 'alarm substance' causes members of a school to scatter rapidly and thus avoid capture by a predator. The possession of such a critical chemical substance is remarkable enough, but the ability to detect it when diluted many hundreds of times in water is even more striking.

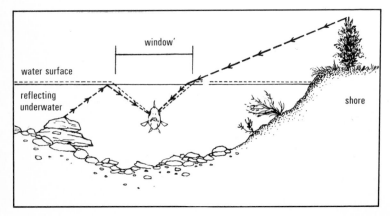

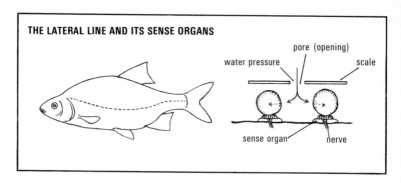

Found almost exclusively in the carp family, this 'alarm substance' is probably particularly important because these fishes live in rather turbid water – due to plant plankton and silt – so they can smell when a member of the school is attacked even if they cannot see it. They also have a special arrangement of vertebrae forming a bony connection between the inner ear and the swimbladder. This accounts for their sharp sense of hearing, and means that they can hear other fish swimming nearby, as well as detect footfalls on the bank and underwater noises. Again, it is a singularly useful ability for fishes living in clouded water.

The lateral line is another sensory system. In most fishes, it can be seen as a line of scales with pores running down the side of the body, but it also extends around the head. The lateral line is a partly covered canal, with special sensory cells which can detect changes in pressure around the fish. The fish uses it to establish whether it is approaching an obstruction or if a predator is nearby, and also whether it is keeping its place in the school. This sense, well-developed in fishes, is found in very few other animals.

Left: a fish underwater can see clearly through the water's surface immediately above it and, because of the way light rays are bent by the air-water surface, can see a good deal on the river bank.
Right: the nostril cavity is provided with a finely divided rosette, richly supplied with nerves, which detect minute traces of scent in the water. Water is pumped through the nostrils continuously so the fish is constantly sampling it.

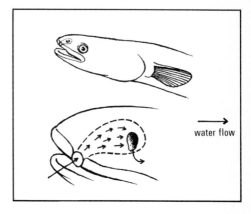

Movement

Life in water is very different to life on land. On land, most vertebrates are confined to a two-dimensional existence, travelling on their two, or four, feet. Only those animals that have escaped to live an aerial life, birds and bats, have anything like the freedom of the three-dimensional life of fishes. But where a bird can soar in the air, a fish must force its way through water – a medium which is heavier and thicker than air. The greater density of water results in fishes adopting all kinds of life styles and body shapes.

Most fishes can swim fast when occasion demands but while some, like the salmon, are capable of sustained fast swimming for days on end, most just sprint for a short while and then rest, or return to gentle swimming. In all fishes which have streamlined, torpedo-shaped bodies, the main propulsive force is the tail with its broad fin at the end. All European freshwater fishes, except for the lampreys, the eel and the flounder, move forwards by beating their tail from side to side, each beat pushing the water back and to one side, which forces the body of the fish forwards. In general, those fishes with deeply-forked tail fins are more powerful swimmers than those with rounded tail fins. The dorsal and anal fins help keep the fish on an even keel; the pectoral and pelvic fins keep it level in the water and enable it to dive and surface.

The lampreys and the eel swim by making a serpentine movement of the body which develops a series of ripples running down its length. The vertical fins on the back and under the tail are held erect and move with the body. The result is that the fish appears to wriggle its way through the water, but if the movement of the body is carefully analyzed, it can be shown that as the ripple runs down the body, it exerts a backward pressure on the water which forces the fish forwards.

The other exception, the flounder, moves by a similar ripple running along the dorsal and anal fins, which in this case lie on the edges of the body. It can also move rapidly for a short distance by beating its tail violently up and down in an approximation of the swimming motion of most fishes.

A third basic type of movement is seen in fishes, like the sticklebacks, which spend much of their lives nearly stationary making only small adjustments to their position in the water by moving their pectoral fins. These fins are large and very flexible paddles with which the fish can turn in any direction and swim slowly backwards and forwards. Most of our freshwater fishes use this means of quiet swimming.

The majority of fishes are roughly the same density as water, which means they are virtually weightless in water. Most have a gas-filled sac in the body cavity, called the swimbladder. Its volume can be altered to make the fish more, or less, dense. As a result, many fishes can hang suspended in the water, using very little energy to stay put. They are one of the few groups of animals which have succeeded in escaping from the burden of the earth's gravity.

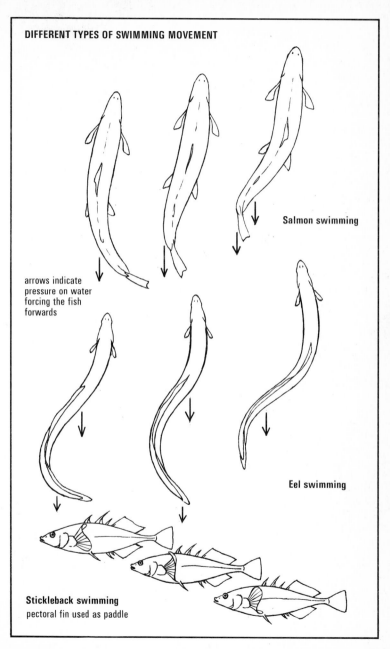

DIFFERENT TYPES OF SWIMMING MOVEMENT

Salmon swimming

arrows indicate
pressure on water
forcing the fish
forwards

Eel swimming

Stickleback swimming
pectoral fin used as paddle

Feeding

As in all ecosystems, the animals and plants of fresh water are bound together in complex interrelationships. One of the relationships is the food web. At its simplest, it can be seen as a chain of organisms which depend on one another for nourishment and growth: fish eat water fleas which eat planktonic algae which are nourished by sunlight and by chemicals in the water. But no fish eat only water fleas, so a series of food chains is needed to show the complex relationships in, say, a pond. Ultimately, everything depends on sunlight and the nutrients in the water which cause algae, diatoms and larger plants to grow. These are eaten by animals of various kinds, and the fishes eat the plant-eating animals, or other animals which are predators. Some fish then eat other fish, and both may be eaten by birds like the heron, kingfisher and osprey, or mammals like the otter and mink.

Although Europe has relatively few freshwater fishes, compared with similar areas in the rest of the world, they have fascinating ways of adapting to the food webs of rivers and lakes. These include different developments of jaws, teeth and gut in the various species. Predators, like the pike and the zander, mostly have large teeth in the jaws and smaller teeth in the roof of the mouth and sometimes on the tongue. They have big mouths and a relatively short gut, and eat fishes almost exclusively once they are longer than about 30 centimetres.

However, the great majority of Europe's fishes are not specialized to eat

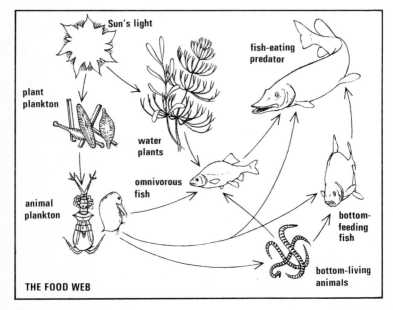

THE FOOD WEB

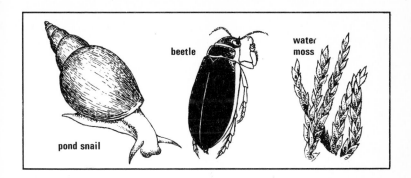

pond snail

beetle

water moss

only one kind of food. None of the members of the carp family have teeth in their jaws or a stomach. Most of them feed on smaller animals and some higher plants. Their jaws can be made to swing forwards so that selecting an edible item is a precise operation. The food then passes to the back of the throat, where it is crushed by the throat teeth against a hard pad resting on the base of the skull. The throat teeth are distinctive in each species, varying in shape, size and number of rows, according to the food the fish eats.

All members of the carp family have similar mouths, but the bream and its close relatives have protrusile jaws with which they can pick up animals buried in the bottom mud. The nases have a hard bony edge to the jaw with which they scrape off algae growing on rocks or timber in the water. The bleak, the rudd and several other species have upward sloping jaws, and it is not surprising to find that much of their food is composed of insects at the surface. Grey mullets, on the other hand, feed mainly on the estuary bed, eating large quantities of mud and sand for the sake of minute crustaceans, worms and other organisms it contains. They have remarkably long intestines, and also a strong-walled stomach in which the food is ground up.

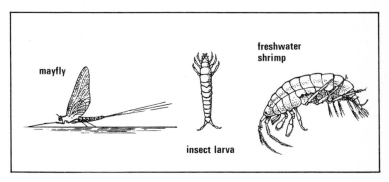

mayfly

freshwater shrimp

insect larva

Breeding

All Europe's native freshwater fishes reproduce by laying eggs. Most breed in schools in open water, over weed beds or over stony bottoms. Muddy bottoms are not usually suitable spawning sites, as the eggs may be buried in the mud, which is often poor in dissolved oxygen and sometimes even gives off the poisonous gas hydrogen sulphide.

In general, the newly shed egg is slightly adhesive and sticks to the plants or stones on which it is laid, and where it develops until hatching. The perch's eggs are an exception, being laid in a lacy mucous thread wound among plant stems or tree roots in the water. Some fishes, like the bullhead and the stone loach, lay their eggs in holes or crevices under stones, rocks, or even in discarded bottles or cans. This protects the eggs, which they guard by fanning them with their fins to aerate them, as well as by keeping egg-eating invertebrates away.

Other fishes build nests to protect their eggs. Salmon and trout both lay their eggs in a hollow in a gravel bed, which the adult makes by boring into the gravel and flicking its tail strongly. The eggs, hidden deep in the gravel, are covered by the river flow washing fine gravel into the nest or by another fish making a nest upstream. Sticklebacks make a nest from

strands of plant matter bound together by mucus from the male's kidneys. Two or three females are usually enticed into the nest, which is irregular in shape and about the size of a golf ball. They lay their eggs and the male fertilizes them and then guards the nest.

A more elaborate breeding behaviour is shown by the bitterling, which lays its eggs in the mantle cavity of a freshwater mussel. The female has a long egg-laying tube with which the eggs are placed inside the mussel, while the male releases his sperm close to the mussel's breathing inlet. The eggs develop inside the mussel and the young fish then escape through the opening from the gills.

The eggs of most fishes develop exposed to the water, so their rate of development depends on the temperature of the water. Trout eggs, which are laid in autumn, and mostly in cold hill streams, may take 160 days to hatch, whereas roach eggs, laid in May or June, will hatch in 5–10 days. In both cases, the development period is nicely timed so that the fry begin to feed when there is an abundance of suitable food for them.

The female perch sheds her spawn in long lacy threads winding in and out of plants and tree roots. This helps normal development by ensuring the eggs get adequate oxygen.

DEVELOPMENT OF THE CARP

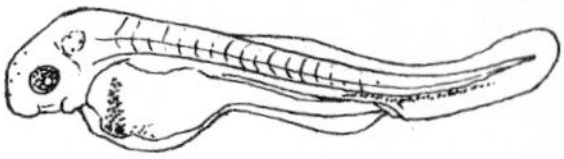

embryo at time of hatching
(5 mm)

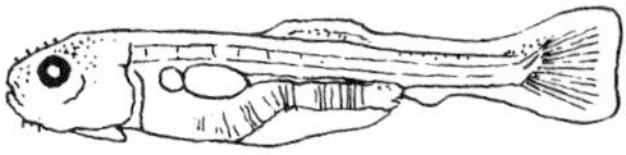

feeding larva 12 days old
(11 mm)

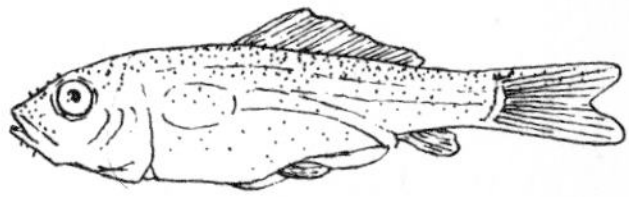

full grown larva 20 days old
(18 mm)

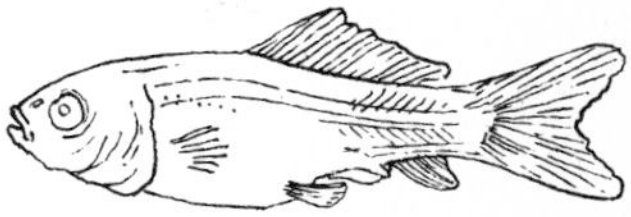

first scales appear (15 mm)

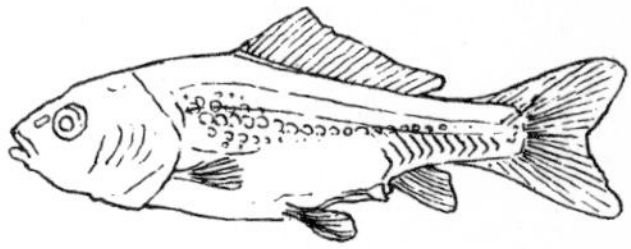

juvenile (22 mm)

Migration

Many fishes migrate, but mostly locally in the river or lake in which they live. However, there are several European species which make very impressive distant migrations. Migrations are essentially linked to two aspects of a fish's life history – breeding and feeding. This is clearly demonstrated by the salmon, which will live in a variety of types of river, as long as they are clean and not too warm, but which needs to lay its eggs in a rather specialized habitat of cold running water, burying them in gravel composed mostly of pea-sized stones. This kind of habitat is usually found well upstream where the river is narrow and the water shallow. Adult salmon could not live for long in such conditions, so, after spawning, those that survive – for most breeding fish die – migrate downstream to the sea.

The small streams form suitable habitats for young salmon, providing sufficient hiding places and adequate food. But even so they begin to drift downstream so that in their second or third year they are living where the river is wider and food resources greater. As bright silvery smolts, they move into the estuary, and soon after out into the sea. Here there is far more food available; large numbers of shrimps, prawns and other crustaceans, and of small fish such as herring, sprat, sand eels and capelin.

MIGRATION ROUTES OF THE SALMON AND THE EEL

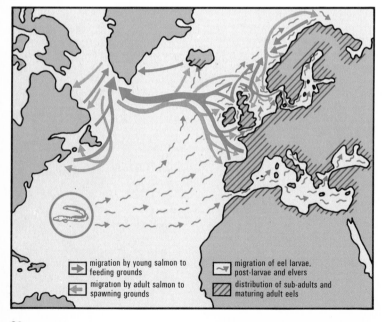

migration by young salmon to feeding grounds

migration by adult salmon to spawning grounds

migration of eel larvae, post-larvae and elvers

distribution of sub-adults and maturing adult eels

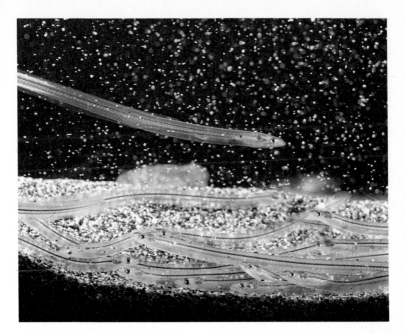

The young salmon grow fast and as they grow become more powerful swimmers and catch larger prey. The salmon's migrations are thus a combination of a feeding migration into the sea, and later a breeding migration back to the river. Sturgeons, shads and, in the north of Europe, trout and charr, all make similar migrations. The freshwater eel behaves in the opposite way, spawning in the sea and migrating virtually across the North Atlantic to Europe's coasts, rivers and lakes, in which it will grow to near maturity. Food resources are scarcer in temperate fresh waters than in the sea, so the eel grows slowly and may live for up to 20 years in fresh water.

Studies of migrations are important to fisheries and various methods are employed to find out

These elvers are in the glass-eel stage, having entered the mouth of the river in which they will grow. Despite their fragile appearance, they have already migrated across the Atlantic and are about 3 years old.

about them. Most of our information has come from tagging a large number of fish with numbered markers. When the fish are recaptured, these markers are returned to the research laboratory and in time yield valuable information about the fishes' migration: where they go, how fast they travel, and how quickly they grow. By using an acoustic tag fastened to the fish and a receiver in a boat, it is possible to track an individual fish. This is mainly used for local studies, for example to establish the route used by salmon through an estuary.

How Fish Survive

The basic strategy of a fish, like any other animal, is to survive long enough to breed and thus start a new generation. To this end, fishes have evolved all kinds of tactics which help them to find food and living places, while avoiding being eaten themselves.

A major consideration, especially among smaller fishes, is to avoid being seen by predators. For this reason, many small species, such as the stone loach and the bullhead, are largely nocturnal. Both also spend most of their time under stones or hidden in plants, the latter a habitat which they share with the sticklebacks and fish like mudminnows. All these species are dull-coloured, which provides a measure of protection by enabling them to blend in with their background.

Coloration is an important method of avoiding detection for larger fishes too. The gudgeon and the barbel are both dull-coloured on the back, often with darker blotches which help break up their outline as they lie with their belly pressed to the river bed. The flounder is even able to blend its colouring to match its background. Predators, such as pike and perch, use their coloration to the opposite effect in trying to stay unobserved by their prey until they are close enough to attack effectively.

Even the brightly shining silvery fishes which are so common in Europe's fresh waters, like many members of the carp family, the shads and the bass, use their coloration to remain inconspicuous. These fishes have greeny brown to dark blue backs which merge gradually into the silvery white sides and belly. Seen from above, their dull backs merge with the coloured water of lowland rivers or the blue of clear lakes; from below their shining silver sides are lost against the reflections of the water's surface.

Living in schools is another defensive tactic which provides protection, especially for young or small fishes. Most young fish live together, even if when full grown they become solitary, but fishes like minnow and dace form schools all their lives. Schooling gives protection in several ways. Firstly, there are many pairs of eyes and sets of defence organs alert in a school, not just one set as in a single fish. So an oncoming predator is quickly detected. Secondly, the individuals in a school are constantly changing their position and it is difficult for a predator to single out one particular fish. Thirdly, if a predator makes a wild random charge at the school, the fish scatter in all directions, again making it hard for the predator to single out any one fish.

Top right: the bleak's silvery sides look conspicuous, but at the surface, where it normally lives, the silver matches the reflections of the surface and helps hide the fish. Right: because of their size minnows can live in very shallow water. They form large schools which protects them from some predators, but exposes them to others.

Using and Protecting Fish

In much of Europe, freshwater fishes are important as food. The Atlantic salmon, the trout, the whitefishes and the larger members of the carp family are well known food fishes; the salmon and the whitefish, when smoked, are gourmet's dishes, as is the caviar obtained from sturgeon. In inland areas, and especially in eastern Europe, the carp, the wels and the zander are particularly important food fishes and make a considerable contribution to the protein available to the human population. The carp is reared in intensive culture in fish farms, along with other species. Fish farming is an important industry, pioneered in Europe, and now widespread in other parts of the world. The carp is native to the Danube basin and parts of Greece, and archaeological discoveries of its bones show that it has been captured and eaten by man for at least 4,000 years in Europe, although its rearing for food is probably only 1,000 years old.

In addition to the value of fish as food, they have enormous recreational value. Within the last two decades, there has been a great increase in the organization of managed fisheries in which fish, mainly rainbow trout and brook charr, sometimes carp, tench and pike, are reared in hatcheries and then released so that anglers can catch them. The sport of angling provides employment in the fishing tackle industry as well as in the management of the waters and associated fish hatcheries. Many of these hatcheries raise fish, notably rainbow trout, for human consumption as well as for stocking purposes.

However, there is no doubt that the human population has had an adverse effect on Europe's freshwater fishes. Adapting watercourses by dredging and straightening the course of lowland rivers has a detrimental effect on the fish fauna, while building weirs for water retention and dams for storage or hydro-electric power is also disruptive. Pollution is another obvious threat to aquatic life. In serious cases it can obliterate the fish even in a major river, either by the discharge of highly toxic chemical waste or by inadequately treated sewage or agricultural waste reaching the river. Chemical waste poisons the animals; sewage and other organic wastes kill them by depriving them of oxygen, because it is used in the bacterial action of breaking down the compounds.

Less dramatic in its effects, but still a serious problem in Europe, is the eutrophication of many lakes and rivers by organic matter. The discharge of enriching substances, particularly those containing nitrates and phosphates, causes plant growth to accelerate and changes the nature of the lake by affecting the balance of life. For the fishes, eutrophication can turn a lake suitable for trout, charr and whitefishes into one better adapted to roach, bream and perch. Many other changes in rivers and lakes tend to a decrease in the sensitive salmon family, the whitefishes and the grayling, and their replacement by pike, perch and members of the carp family. Among these is the acid rain which falls when sulphur rich fuels are burnt by industry.

There is clearly a great need for the protection of many species, and this could best be accomplished by the protection of the habitats in which they live. Many highland lakes have unique populations of charr and whitefish, rivers and lakes in Greece and Yugoslavia are the home of numerous unique species, while the wetlands around the southern Spanish coastline have the unique Valencia toothcarp. Such habitats should have a high priority for conservation, and there are many other fishes which urgently need protection throughout Europe.

Rubbish and dead fish at the pool's surface are a sure sign of pollution. Some waters are polluted with toxic industrial effluents, but most pollution is the result of organic matter, particularly sewage, decomposing and using all the oxygen in the water.

LAMPREY FAMILY
Petromyzonidae

Lampreys are a group of fish-like vertebrates which, because they spend part – or all – of their lives in fresh water, and look superficially like eels, are usually included with fishes. They lack jaws, have only gristle in their skeletons, and no vertebrae, although they do possess a notochord. Instead of jaws, they have a flat disc on the underside of the head. In the larvae, this disc has a filtering function, while in the adult it often has sharp teeth by means of which the lampreys inflict wounds on fishes and suck their blood. Instead of a gill opening on either side of the head protected by gill covers, as in true fishes, lampreys have a series of seven separate holes along the side behind the head.

There are 38 living species of lamprey in the world, which together with the rather more numerous marine hagfishes, comprise the superclass Agnatha, the sole representatives of a group of abundant animals now mostly extinct. Most of them live in the northern hemisphere, though a few species are known from western South America, southern Australia and New Zealand. Only eight species live in Europe, although others are found to the east, around the Caspian Sea for example. Only two of these species migrate to the sea to feed.

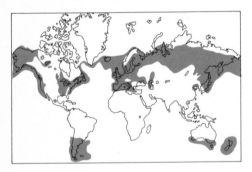

Lampreys and their relatives live in cool temperate zones; some are migratory and move into the sea to feed, but all spawn in fresh water.

LAMPREY SUCKERS

Sea lamprey

Brook lamprey

Danube lamprey

Zanandrea's lamprey

River lamprey

Sea Lamprey

SEA LAMPREY
Petromyzon marinus
90 cm. Adults are heavily blotched dark green, grey or black on back and sides; yellowish-white ventrally. Dorsal fins widely spaced. Teeth in sucker strong, conical, except in centre where they are sharply pointed; the lower tooth plate with 7-9 pointed cusps.

Distribution: found around the Atlantic seaboard of Europe from the White Sea to Portugal, and in the western Mediterranean and Adriatic. Also on the North American Atlantic coast.

Natural history: a migratory lamprey which breeds in rivers March-May, laying its clear eggs in nests of gravel. After hatching the young, known as prides, live buried in silt for 2-5 years feeding on the diatoms and minute animals which they filter from the river mud. Migrating to the sea, the lamprey spends 3-4 years as a parasite of fish in the sea and estuary, sucking their blood. It can be a serious pest to valuable food fish. In winter it returns to the river to spawn and adults all die after spawning. The sea lamprey is uncommon in places due to the interruption of its migration up river by weirs and pollution.

DANUBE LAMPREY
Eudontomyzon danfordi
25 cm. Uniform pale golden brown on back and sides; creamy ventrally. Body deepest in middle; dorsal fins widely spaced. Teeth in mouth sucker strong and pointed, three tooth plates on the ventral side, the innermost with 9-13 sharp points, the centre one the longest.

Distribution: confined to the River Danube, where it lives in the smaller tributaries.

Natural history: migrates only locally within the river of its birth. The larvae live for 3-4 years in muddy patches feeding on micro-organisms. They metamorphose in summer and the sub-adults are parasitic, feeding on many kinds of fishes and amphibians. They fast through the winter, feed again during the warm seasons and breed the following spring. After this, the adults die. Spawning takes place April-May on sandy banks with shingle, male and female both hollowing out a nest in which the eggs are buried in sand by the current and by other lampreys spawning nearby.

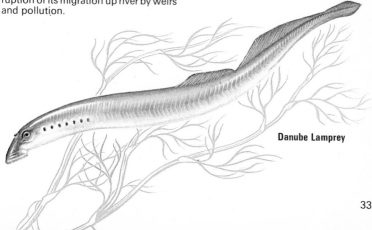

Danube Lamprey

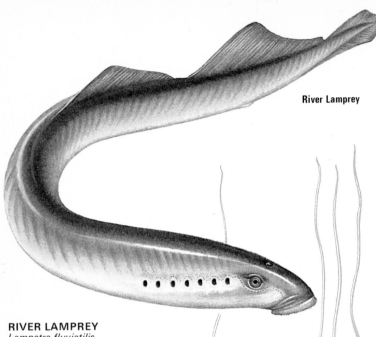

River Lamprey

RIVER LAMPREY
Lampetra fluviatilis
50 cm. Uniformly coloured, with a greeny-brown back, yellowish sides and a whitish belly. Dorsal fins widely spaced, second dorsal fin almost joined to tail fin. Teeth in mouth sucker few, but sharply pointed; lower tooth plate with 7-10 pointed cusps.

Distribution: widely distributed in western Europe, along the Atlantic coast except for Norway. Not found in the Danube basin. Occurs in Spain, France and northern Italy

Natural history: a migratory lamprey which spawns in rivers March-May, both sexes making a nest in shingle in running water for the eggs, which number 19-20,000 per female. The adults die after spawning, but the larvae live in muddy stream beds for 3-5 years before metamorphosis at 14-15 cm length. The sub-adults migrate to the sea (or a large lake in inland areas) where they feed parasitically on fishes. After 2-3 years, they return to the river, mainly in autumn or early winter and migrate upstream to their spawning grounds. The river lamprey is now uncommon locally due to pollution and the damming of rivers.

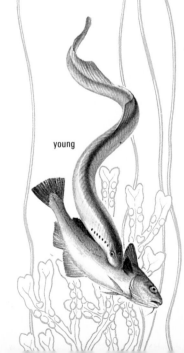

young

34

BROOK LAMPREY
Lampetra planeri

25 cm. Dark brown to slate grey above, merging gradually into yellowish sides and creamy-white belly. The adults have dorsal fins joined together at their bases; the second dorsal is joined to the tail by a low ridge. Mouth sucker with weak blunt teeth, the posterior tooth plate with only 6-9 weakly rounded cusps.

Distribution: widely spread in the Atlantic, Baltic and North Sea rivers of western Europe, from northern Sweden to France, but not continuously distributed, as its range is divided up into small pockets.

Natural history: a non-migratory lamprey which lives in small streams and the upper reaches of rivers. Its larvae live buried in soft mud in these streams for 3-5 years, feeding on micro-organisms. They metamorphose into adults in winter, but the adults do not feed nor are they parasitic. They breed March-April in nests dug in shallow water in tributary streams and ditches, laying 850-1400 eggs per female. The adults die after spawning.

ZANANDREA'S LAMPREY
Lampetra zanandreai

18 cm. Grey brown above, pale brown on the sides and creamy ventrally. It is very similar to the Brook lamprey, and has been regarded as a subspecies of it. It has fewer myomeres (muscle blocks) in its body (52-60), and the teeth are fewer and smaller (5 cusps in the posterior tooth plate and 2, instead of 3, on each side).

Distribution: lives in the River Po system in northern Italy, and probably in other rivers on the Adriatic coast, but its range is not well known. This lamprey replaces the Brook lamprey in Italy.

Natural history: a non-migratory lamprey which spawns in spring on sand and pebble-bottomed streams in the upper tributaries of the river. Its larvae spend 2-3 years burrowing in mud in small streams where ripples and deeper slow stretches alternate, the mud at the tail of the pools being its main habitat. After the young metamorphose, the adults do not feed but, fasting through the next winter, they spawn in the spring and then die.

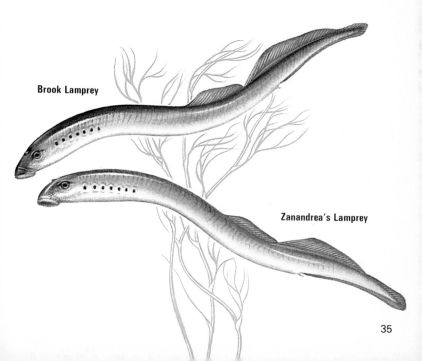

Brook Lamprey

Zanandrea's Lamprey

STURGEON FAMILY
Acipenseridae

Sturgeons are fishes belonging to the Chondrostei, a group of primitive fishes which have jaws, scales, and rays in their fins. Apart from another family, the paddlefishes, known only from China and the United States, all the other members of the group are fossil forms. Sturgeons therefore can be regarded as living fossils. They are distinguished by the five rows of large bony scutes running along their bodies, the tail fin upper lobe being much longer than the lower. Their skeletons are made of gristle (cartilage) not bone, and the lower intestine has a special spiral section which increases its absorbative area greatly, but not its bulk. Sturgeons are confined to the northern hemisphere. They breed in fresh water, and migrate downstream afterwards, and as the young grow. Several species migrate into the sea on a feeding migration that lasts several years. There are 23 known kinds of sturgeon in the world.

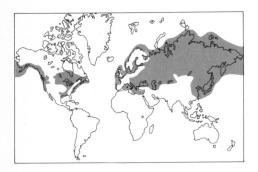

Members of the sturgeon family breed in fresh water, but some species, especially the larger ones, migrate to the sea to feed. Some 23 species are recognized.

Sturgeon

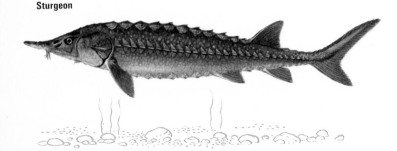

STURGEON
Acipenser sturio
3·5 m. The bony plates on the sides are large and their bases barely touch; lateral rows have 26-36 plates, rows on the belly 9-13 up to the vent. Snout long, with 2 pairs of long smooth barbels midway between its tip and the mouth, which is small.

Distribution: occurs in the Baltic Sea, and the Atlantic Ocean from Norway southwards to North Africa. Also in the western Mediterranean, the northern part of the eastern Mediterranean, and the Black Sea. Enters rivers anywhere in that range, but is now rare – due to pollution and obstructions in rivers.

Natural history: a migratory sturgeon which in the sea lives near the bottom in moderately shallow water, where it eats molluscs, worms, crustaceans and bottom-living fishes. May stay in the sea up to 6 years before returning to fresh water to spawn in deep gravel-bottomed rivers April-May. Female lays 800,000-2,400,000 eggs, depending on her size. The small sticky black eggs are swept over the gravel, to which they adhere. They hatch in up to 7 days and the young fish spend up to 3 years in the river before migrating. The sturgeon is very rare in Atlantic Europe, being found in fresh water only in Lake Ladoga (near Leningrad), in the French River Gironde and in the Spanish Guadalquivir.

ADRIATIC STURGEON
Acipenser naccari
2 m. Bony plates on the sides are large and very conspicuous, more than twice as deep as they are wide; 40-42 plates on each side, 12-14 in a line along the back. The snout is blunt but moderately pointed, and the two pairs of barbels, which are smooth and rather long, are placed closer to the snout tip than the mouth.

Distribution: occurs only in the Adriatic Sea and its rivers. Virtually confined to Italy in the rivers Po and Adige and the streams of Lombardy and Veneto.

Natural history: a migratory fish, spawning in fresh water, then moving downstream till it comes to the sea where it feeds and becomes sexually mature. Spawns April-May in the deep water of the river, usually over a gravel bed. The young fish spend at least the first year of their lives in fresh water feeding on bottom-living invertebrates before migrating. The Adriatic sturgeon has now become extremely rare, and its range both in the sea and in rivers has decreased. As its natural history is virtually unknown, it is difficult to propose conservation measures to help it survive. It is one of Europe's vulnerable species.

Adriatic Sturgeon

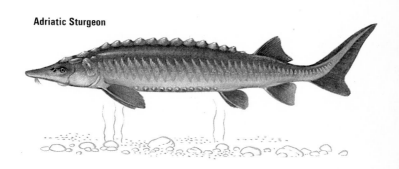

SHIP STURGEON
Acipenser nudiventris
2 m. More than 60 small, rather sharply pointed, bony plates on the sides; 12-15 plates on the back. The lower lip is continuous (other sturgeons have a distinct break in this lip); the barbels on the underside of the snout have fine branches on their inner sides.
Distribution: inhabits northern rivers of the Black Sea and those on the western edge of the Caspian Sea. Travels up the Danube as far as Budapest (Hungary).
Natural history: a migratory sturgeon which spawns in rivers, usually on pebble bottoms in the deep water of the middle reaches, March-May. Female lays between 200,000 and 1,250,000 eggs, according to her size. The young hatch in 5-10 days and move slowly downstream, reaching the sea in winter, although some will spend a year on the journey. It is 12-14 years before this fish is sexually mature, during which period it lives in the sea, feeding mainly on bottom-living invertebrates. A valuable commercial sturgeon both for meat and for caviare, but now rare and in need of conservation measures.

STERLET
Acipenser ruthenus
1·2 m. Similar to other sturgeons, but with a more pointed, upturned snout, and with very long barbels which are finely branched along half their length. 60-70 small bony plates on the sides; 12-16 on the back and on the undersides. Plates on the sides conspicuously light-coloured, forming a whitish stripe down each side.
Distribution: lives in rivers running into the northern Black Sea and Caspian Sea, and also in the Arctic rivers of the USSR. In Europe it is virtually confined to the Danube and the Volga.
Natural history: this is a wholly freshwater sturgeon, though it does penetrate to estuarine water in the Danube and the Caspian Sea. It spawns April-June on clean, stony river beds after a short upstream migration. The young lie in the gravel for a few days after hatching, then disperse into shallow water, while the adults move into deeper water downstream.

STELLATE STURGEON
Acipenser stellatus
1·5 m. A slim-looking sturgeon with a very elongate and upturned snout. 30-40 bony plates on sides; 12-16 on back.
Distribution: lives in the basins of the Black Sea, Sea of Azov and the Caspian Sea, and in the rivers entering the northern and western sides of these seas. Reported in the last century in the Adriatic where it may now be extinct.
Natural history: The most common sturgeon in the easternmost parts of Europe, but less so in the Danube where it is rare and found only as far upstream as Slovakia. An important commercial species. Migrates into rivers from the sea in either August-September or March-June (depending on the river) and spawns May-September over gravel to which eggs adhere. 20,000-360,000 eggs are laid by each female and they hatch in 4-5 days. Within a few hours of hatching, the larvae rise to the surface and are carried downstream. They enter the sea at 2-3 months and will return as adults aged 8-12 years. Feeds mainly on bottom-living invertebrates, but adults eat fishes.

BELUGA
Huso huso
5 m. A huge heavy-bodied sturgeon with a black back and a creamy-white belly which is sharply defined by the 40-60 bony plates on the sides. 11-15 plates on the back; 9-12 small plates on the belly. Mouth very wide and crosses from side to side. Two pairs of long barbels on the snout.
Distribution: widespread in the Caspian, Black and Adriatic Seas and the rivers which run into them. Migrates upstream in the Danube as far as Bratislava.
Natural history: a migratory fish spawning in May well upstream in rivers, on gravel bottoms to which the eggs stick. Some spawn in the mouths of rivers. After hatching, the young fish move downstream and enter the sea when only a few months old. Sexual maturity is attained at 14 years in males and 18 years in females, and this time is spent in the sea. Feeds mainly on fishes, though the young eat some bottom-living invertebrates.

Ship Sturgeon

Sterlet

Stellate Sturgeon

Beluga

HERRING FAMILY
Clupeidae

The herring family comprises a very large number of marine fishes which live mainly in coastal waters, usually near the surface, but a number of species enter fresh water to breed. Most members of the herring family are small (only a few species grow longer than 40 cm), and they are particularly abundant in tropical and warm temperate regions. They are rather slender–bodied fishes, covered with thin and easily detached scales; they have a single dorsal fin, and no spines in their fins. Most of their food is minute plankton captured by the fine mesh of gill rakers on the gill arches in the throat. They have small teeth and protrusile jaws.

ALLIS SHAD
Alosa alosa
60 cm. Deep-bodied and large-headed. The body is covered with large silvery scales but the head is naked. Gill covers have ridges radiating from the eye. The 80-130 brownish gill rakers on the first gill arch (seen by lifting the gill cover up vertically) are as long as the blood red gill filaments. There is a deep notch in the mid-line of the upper jaw.

Distribution: along the European coastline from Norway to North Africa and in the western Mediterranean.

Natural history: a migratory fish which enters river mouths in spring and swims upstream in schools to spawning grounds in swiftly-flowing reaches. Spawns in May at night with much splashing and disturbance. The eggs sink into the gravel river bed, hatching in 4-8 days according to the temperature. The adults return to the sea. Much reduced in numbers due to pollution, dams, navigation locks, and weirs in rivers, the Allis Shad is scarce in most of northern Europe. The adults feed on planktonic crustaceans and fish in the sea; they do not usually feed in fresh water.

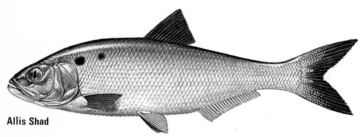

Allis Shad

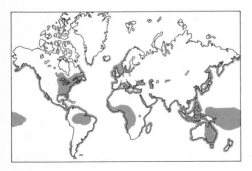

There are around 180 species in this family, mostly inshore marine fishes, some of great economic importance. Several species, mainly the shads, migrate into fresh water to breed.

40

TWAITE SHAD
Alosa fallax
55 cm. A large-headed, herring-like fish, with a sharp keel on its belly. Deep body, fully scaled with large, silvery, easily detached scales; head scaleless. Gill covers ridged with radiating lines from the eye; deep notch in mid-line of the upper jaw. A series of black blotches of decreasing size runs from top of gill cover to level with dorsal fin – a useful but not absolute identifying feature. 40-60 gill rakers on the first gill arch, shorter than the blood red gill filaments.

Distribution: around the whole European coastline from Iceland and southern Norway south to North Africa; in Baltic, Mediterranean and Black Seas.

Natural history: migratory, this shad enters many of the rivers in its range to spawn in the lower reaches just about the limit of tidal influence. A number of populations live entirely in fresh water in Lake Killarney (Ireland) and the north Italian lakes. Feeds on crustaceans and small freshwater fishes but in the sea eats sand eels, sprats and young herring. Does not feed during spawning migration.

BLACK SEA SHAD
Caspialosa pontica
50 cm. Slender, with a moderately large head. Body fully scaled and head naked; the gill covers have ridges radiating from the eye. A deep notch in the mid-line of the upper jaw. Teeth small but well developed, in a patch on the roof of the mouth. 70-80 gill rakers on the first gill arch.

Distribution: lives only in the Black Sea, migrating into the rivers Danube, Dniester, Dnieper and Don to spawn. A closely related subspecies lives in the Caspian Sea and spawns in its rivers.

Natural history: migratory, overwinters in the southern parts of the Black Sea, moving northwards in spring to arrive at river mouths mostly in late April. Spawns upstream in schools, late June-July, in protected backwaters and eddies. Spawning mostly takes place in the twilight, morning and evening. The eggs float, hatching in about 40 hours, and the fry are carried downstream by the current although some take shelter in areas where the flow is minimal. Adults move downstream after spawning. Young fish eat crustaceans and insect larvae.

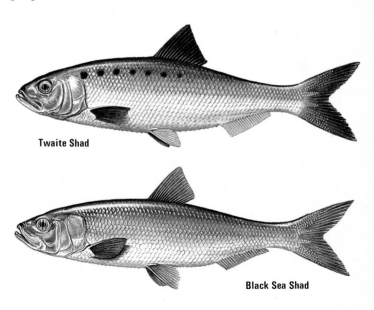

Twaite Shad

Black Sea Shad

EEL FAMILY
Anguillidae

As a rule eels are marine fishes and there are nearly 600 species known worldwide. However, about 15 species belonging to this family are known as freshwater eels, although they all spawn in the sea. Eels are slender-bodied animals, lacking pelvic fins, while their dorsal and anal fins are fused with the tail fin to form a continuous fringe. Although some marine eels, like the snipe eels, appear to be active and free-swimming, most live in close contact with the bottom, either hiding in crevices in rock or coral, or burrowing into the bottom mud – a habitat suited to their sinuous shape, absence of spiny fins, and scaleless (or apparently scaleless) skins. Freshwater eels are patchily distributed, in the North Atlantic both in North America and Europe, and in the Indian and West Pacific Oceans. The two Atlantic species are closely related, the only easily established differences between them being in the number of vertebrae and fin rays. Like all eels their larvae are transparent and shaped like a willow leaf, and float in the ocean near the surface. This type of larva is known as a leptocephalus – a name that was proposed when it was thought to be a distinct type of fish. The European eel larvae make the crossing from the spawning grounds near Bermuda in three years; it takes the larvae of the American eel only one year from spawning ground to river.

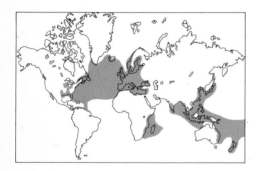

The 15 or so species which make up the eel family live in fresh water but migrate to the sea to spawn. Details of the spawning areas of the Pacific and Indian Ocean species are poorly known.

Eel

EEL
Anguilla anguilla

1 m. Elongate; cylindrical body with a small gill opening, rounded pectoral fins, dorsal fin and anal fin joined with the tail fin round the tip of the tail. The origin of the dorsal fin is closer to the vent than the gill openings. Head and body extremely slimy, which conceals the minute scales embedded in the skin at right angles. Lower jaw longer than upper jaw. Young and immature eels dull brown with a greenish hue on the back and upper sides, yellow on the belly; maturing eels, which have begun their spawning migration, dark on the back and silvery or white ventrally.

Distribution: throughout northern and western Europe including the Mediterranean basin and Black Sea. Lives on the coasts from Iceland and central Norway southwards to North Africa; also in rivers, lakes and ponds. The larvae range the Atlantic from near Bermuda to the European coastline, including the Mediterranean. Many freshwater eels never come into fresh water, spending all their lives on the shore and in estuaries.

Natural history: eels in fresh water are in the feeding and developing stage of their lives, preceded by a 3-year juvenile stage at sea and followed by a transatlantic migration to their spawning grounds. While in fresh water they live in any body of water to which they can gain access, migrating across land from the rivers (usually during rainy nights). They lie buried in mud and feed, mostly at night, on bottom-living insect larvae, crustaceans and small fishes. Although often accused of feeding on trout and salmon eggs, eels do very little harm in this way, though to some extent they do compete with the young trout for food. Freshwater eels live in rivers and lakes for 8-15 years before changing colour as they mature and beginning their seaward migration. The eyes increase in size, the gut shrinks and the reproductive organs begin to develop. They probably do not feed as they make their way to the spawning grounds.

These fragile transparent elvers have just arrived in the river mouth after a transatlantic migration lasting 3 years.

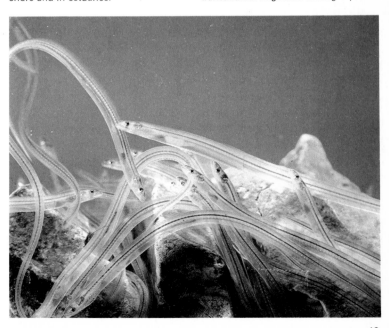

PIKE FAMILY
Esocidae

Pikes are fishes of the northern hemisphere, with the European species also being found in North America, where it is called the northern pike. North America also has the larger muskellunge *(Esox masquinongy)* and two smaller species known as pickerels, while in Siberia the Amur pike *(Esox reicherti)* is nearly as large as the European pike. All these fishes have long, slender, fully-scaled bodies, and scaleless heads.

PIKE
Esox lucius

1·5 m. Body long but rounded; large scaleless head. Long pointed jaws with big sharp teeth in lower jaws only. The eyes, placed high on the side of the head, are moderately large, and a shallow groove runs up each side of the snout in front of the eye. Dorsal and anal fins are opposite, close to tail fin. Colour variable, usually dark greenish-brown, the sides flecked and barred with cream, yellow or golden marks. Bold dark bars on posterior fins. The body markings and those on the tail are unique to each individual fish and persist over several years, if not for life.

Distribution: across Europe, except for mountainous regions. Absent from Greece and the Balkans, Italy except for the north, and Spain and Portugal.

Natural history: lives in slowly-flowing lowland rivers and lakes, particularly those with submerged plants. The pike waits in ambush in the plants – its colouring is very effective camouflage – then makes a lightning charge at passing prey. Most of its hunting is done by sight and thus in daylight, but it has a series of large sensory pores on the lower jaws which help it detect prey at night. When moderately large, the pike feeds mainly on fishes but will occasionally eat frogs, water voles and ducklings. When young, it eats aquatic insect larvae, crustaceans and small fishes. Spawning takes place February-May, the female usually being accompanied by two or even three smaller males. The eggs are laid in shallow water over

Pike

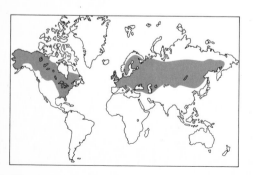

Three species in eastern North America, one in Siberia, and the pike, which is circumpolar, comprise the family. The pike has been introduced to parts of Europe where it is not native.

plants and stick to the leaves, hatching in 10-15 days. The young stay stuck to the plants for several days after hatching. A female lays 16,000-75,000 eggs. The young become sexually mature at 3-4 years; males live for 7-10 years, females up to 25 years.

MUDMINNOW FAMILY
Umbridae

Though closely related to the pikes, the mudminnows are much less widely distributed. They are tiny fishes (never longer than 20 cm), rather stubby, with a large blunt head. Dorsal and anal fins are far back near the tail fin; pelvic fins far down the body. Head and body have large scales with a distinctively etched surface. Mudminnows can live in small waters, often with very low dissolved oxygen levels; and one North American species can reputedly stand being frozen in the ice for long periods. There are five members of the family, only one of which is native to Europe.

EUROPEAN MUDMINNOW
Umbra krameri
13 cm. Stout-bodied with a large head; scales on gill cover and cheek. The eye is moderately large. The dorsal fin, originating above the pelvic fin base, has 14 rays. (The North American Eastern mudminnow, which has been introduced to western Europe, has fewer dorsal rays).
Distribution: confined to the basin of the Danube between Vienna and the Black Sea, and the lower reaches of the Dniester.
Natural history: lives in overgrown swamps, backwaters of rivers, oxbow lakes and irrigation canals – all waters in which dissolved oxygen is often low in summer. Feeds on bottom-living insect larvae, crustaceans and molluscs, and also eats near-surface animals. Spawns in spring, laying rather more than 150 eggs in a nest in a hollow in the river bottom which the female guards, protecting them from predators and ensuring that they do not become smothered by silt. The female also removes any dead or diseased eggs. The eggs hatch in 4-5 days.

European Mudminnow

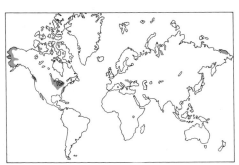

A family of only 5 species, mostly found in North America. One of these, the eastern mudminnow, Umbra pygmaea, *has been introduced to western Europe.*

WHITEFISH FAMILY
Coregonidae

The whitefishes or ciscoes are a large group of northern hemisphere fishes related to the salmon family. They are silvery-brown or grey in colour, with comparatively large scales (fewer in number than the salmons), a rather short-based dorsal fin, and an adipose fin between the rayed dorsal and the tail fins. They usually have small jaws, and most have no teeth in the jaws. Whitefishes are mainly freshwater fishes, confined in Europe to mountain lakes in the south (Alps) and west (British Isles) of their range, but in northern Europe they live in lakes and rivers, as well as migrating out to sea in the far north. They are extremely difficult to identify, partly because the features usually employed in the identification of fishes vary considerably in whitefishes from habitat to habitat. Fish of one distinct type, introduced to a new habitat, will produce very different fish – in number of scales, body shape, and number of gill rakers – in only a few generations.

Whitefishes and ciscoes are enormously important commercial fishes in inland parts of Europe, as well as in North America; their flesh is slightly oily and well flavoured, and they are superb when smoked. Because of their importance, they have been stocked in many natural as well as man-made lakes, but several natural populations have declined due to pollution – especially increased acidity – and overfishing.

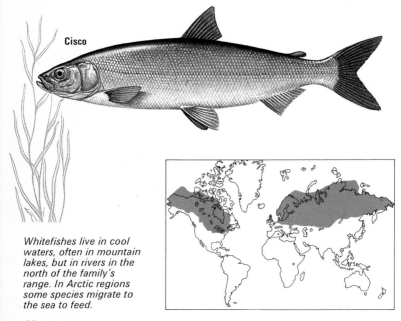

Cisco

Whitefishes live in cool waters, often in mountain lakes, but in rivers in the north of the family's range. In Arctic regions some species migrate to the sea to feed.

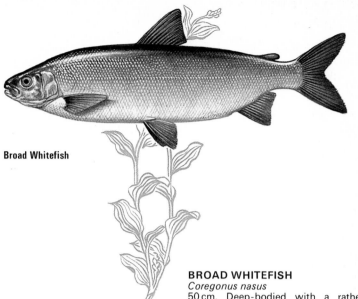

Broad Whitefish

CISCO or VENDACE
Coregonus albula
35 cm. Slightly deeper-bodied than most whitefishes with a curved belly and an almost straight back. The curved lower jaw protrudes in front of the snout making the mouth oblique. 36-52 gill rakers on the first gill arch.
Distribution: widely distributed in the Baltic Sea basin; also occurs in the Lake District in England and in south-west Scotland (Vendace), as well as the Alpine lakes and the River Volga basin.
Natural history: migratory in the rivers of the Baltic Sea, moving down to the sea in winter after spawning in October-December. The eggs are laid over gravel beds in depths of 2-3 m and overwinter in the gravel, taking 100-120 days to hatch. Lake populations spawn in shallows near the lake edge, often in river mouths running into the lake, but most of their lives are spent in deep water. Often stunted due to poor food supply, they lay only 1,000-6,000 eggs; river spawners are more fecund. Most populations feed heavily on planktonic molluscs and larger crustaceans.

BROAD WHITEFISH
Coregonus nasus
50 cm. Deep-bodied with a rather humped back. Snout blunt and rather humped before the eye, mouth small, upper jawbone deep and short. 20-29, usually 22, gill rakers on the first gill arch.
Distribution: widely distributed from the basin of the Baltic across Arctic USSR to Siberia, and then into Alaska and northernmost Canada. Lake populations in the Alps.
Natural history: lives in cold deep lakes, and in rivers running into the Arctic Ocean. In the latter it migrates upriver during summer to breed in October-November; in lakes it spawns close inshore but often in deep water. The water temperature at spawning is about 2-3°C. Each female produces 10,000-30,000 eggs, depending on her size, but lake populations are smaller and lay fewer eggs. Sexual maturity is attained at 4-5 years and the Broad Whitefish may live for up to 10 years. It feeds mainly on bottom-living larvae, molluscs and crustaceans. In the Arctic this is an important food fish and it is artificially propagated in hatcheries. Most of the lake populations of western Europe are threatened by eutrophication or pollution.

COMMON WHITEFISH or POWAN

Coregonus lavaretus
70 cm. Head and body variable in shape. Some populations have bluntly rounded snouts, in others the snout is pointed. Mouth moderately large (either terminal or slightly ventral), the upper jawbone reaching back as far as the front of the eye. 25-34 gill rakers on first arch.

Distribution: widespread across northern Europe from the Baltic basin to the USSR. Also occurs in lakes in north-west England, Wales and south-west Scotland, the Alps, and lakes of the Volga.

Natural history: extremely variable in its choice of habitats. Some populations are confined to lakes, but to the north it lives in rivers and migrates to coastal waters to feed. Some lake populations spawn on gravelly shallows, as do most riverine stocks; others lay their eggs on sand in deep water. All spawn in November-December; the number of eggs per female varying between 1,000-28,000 according to size. Lake fish are smaller and thus lay fewer eggs. Feeds on planktonic crustaceans, but as it grows eats insect larvae and larger crustaceans. Estuarine whitefish feed heavily on crustaceans. An important food fish in much of northern Europe, heavily fished inland.

Much scarcer in many lakes due to eutrophication, predation and competition with introduced fishes.

HOUTING

Coregonus oxyrinchus
50 cm. Very variable in body shape but tends to be more slender than most whitefishes. In the typical form, the snout protrudes to a fleshy point. 35-44 gill rakers on the first gill arch.

Distribution: occurs in lakes in the Baltic basin and migrates into the rivers of Scandinavia to breed, thence across northern USSR. At one time occurred in the North Sea and was found in estuaries and rivers of the Netherlands, Germany and Denmark (and rarely on the English coast), but this stock now seems to be extinct.

Natural history: in the Baltic migrates up river to spawn over gravel beds in the lower reaches of rivers, October-January. Young stay in the river 3-4 months after hatching, then migrate to the sea. They become sexually mature in 3-4 years. At first they feed mostly on planktonic crustaceans, changing to bottom-living animals, chiefly crustaceans and molluscs as they grow. Much uncertainty surrounds the differences between this and the Common Whitefish, and they may prove to be extreme forms of the same species complex.

Common Whitefish

Houting

GRAYLING FAMILY
Thymallidae

The graylings are close relatives of both the whitefishes and the salmons. Although some authorities recognize the three groups as subfamilies within the salmonid family, the differences between them seem sufficient to regard them as three distinct families. Four species of grayling are recognized, two found in the Far East, one in North America, and the fourth in Europe. All have a high, many-rayed dorsal fin, with a secondary adipose fin between the dorsal and the tail. They have moderately large scales, arranged in distinct rows, and a scaleless head. The mouth is rather small, and although there are teeth on the upper jawbone they are small. Graylings are said to smell of the herb thyme, which is the reason for their scientific name; it is not, however, a strong scent.

GRAYLING
Thymallus thymallus
60 cm. Clearly distinguished by the long-based dorsal fin with 17-24 rays, each long and branched, and the adipose fin on the back. Males have longer dorsal fin rays than females, with an orange-red margin on the free edge. Young grayling have dusky blotches along their sides (parr marks) as do trout and salmon, but also have the large dorsal fin.
Distribution: England and Wales, and across western Europe, south to central France, north of the Alps and in the Danube.
Natural history: a river fish living in clear, cool, well-oxygenated water, and in some lakes especially in mountainous areas. Requires good quality water and is now rare in much of its range due to pollution. Breeds in spring in gravel shallows in a nest cut by the female in the gravel. The male displays to the female before spawning and, during spawning, wraps his dorsal fin over her back to ensure that sperm and eggs are not washed out of the nest by the current. The eggs hatch in 3-4 weeks and the young mature at 3-4 years. Grayling feed on bottom-living insect larvae, crustaceans and molluscs.

Grayling

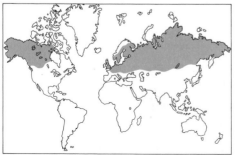

A family of only four species: two in Mongolia, one in Asia and North America, and one in Europe. They are all confined to cool, clean fresh water, both rivers and lakes.

49

SALMON FAMILY
Salmonidae

In the present restricted sense, this family comprises the salmons, found in the Atlantic and Pacific Oceans and their borderlands, the various kinds of trout, and the charrs. The Salmonidae is widely distributed in the northern hemisphere, and many salmon and trout, because of their economic and sporting value, have been widely redistributed and now live in parts of South America, southern Africa, Australia and New Zealand. Salmon family members are medium to large fishes with slender bodies, fully scaled with small to very small scales, but with naked heads. None of their fins have spines in them. They have a single dorsal fin with rays in it approximately halfway along the back, and an adipose fin, which lacks rays, between the dorsal fin and the tail fin. The pectoral fins are set low-down behind the head; the pelvic fins are far along the belly, beneath the dorsal fin.

The salmonids are freshwater fishes in that they all breed in fresh water, although many make a feeding migration to the sea and return when they are sexually mature. The sea-going habit is more pronounced to the north – all the Salmonidae in Arctic rivers migrate – while towards the southern extremity of their range most are entirely freshwater fishes. Many of these southern populations are confined to the lakes or river systems they colonized during periods of extension of polar ice, and in which they have become trapped by rising sea temperatures. Over the succeeding thousands of years, these populations have evolved from the successive migratory forms into recognizably distinct stocks. This is due to differences in the individual environments in which they live and also to their genetic isolation. It is most obvious in Europe in the Arctic charr which live in a hundred or more isolated mountain lakes. Each population can be shown to be slightly different, and most of them very different, from the migratory, river-living form of northern Scandinavia, Iceland and the USSR, which is close to the migratory presumed ancestral form.

The salmon is the most notable migratory fish in Europe (see map). Feeding in Greenland, it returns to the headwaters of European rivers to spawn, often leaping almost insurmountable obstacles (right).

Salmon

male

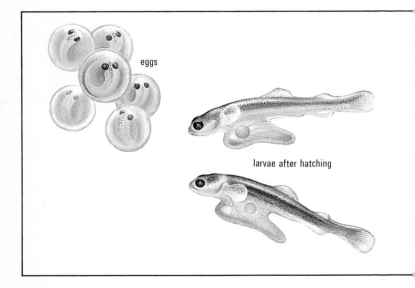
eggs

larvae after hatching

SALMON
Salmo salar
1·5 m. Streamlined with a slender body and pointed head, only slightly compressed at the sides and deepest at the dorsal fin origin. Upper jawbone extends to the level of the back part of the eye, not further. Body narrow in front of the tail fin (caudal peduncle); upper and lower rays stand out clearly from the outline. 10-13 scales between base of adipose fin and lateral line. 15-20 slender gill rakers on first arch. Coloration very variable, young salmon migrating to the sea are green or blue on the back and brilliantly silvery with x-shaped black spots mostly above the lateral line. After being in fresh water for a while, they become dark on the back with reddish sides (males also develop a strongly hooked lower jaw). Young fish are dark above with a series of 8-11 dark smudges on their sides; edge of adipose fin grey.
Distribution: along the Atlantic coastline from northern Spain to northern Norway, Iceland and the Baltic countries, and on the North American coast. Migrates across Atlantic to the coast of Greenland. The salmon is now rare to the south of its range and on North Sea coasts.

female

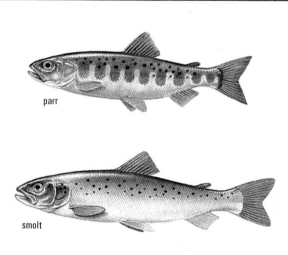

parr

smolt

Natural history: spawns in the headwaters of rivers mostly in November and December, the female making a hollow in the gravel bed. Into this 'redd' the eggs are laid and fertilized by the male, although commonly the larger fish are joined by young but sexually active smaller males which join in the spawning. The eggs, 5-7 mm in diameter, sink into the gravel, and are buried by other salmon spawning upstream, or by the stream gradually filling in the nest. They hatch April-May, but live in the gravel for about one month, nourished by the yolk of the egg. Around midsummer they begin to feed on small crustaceans; later on insect larvae. Young salmon spend up to three years in their natal stream before moving downstream to the sea. This is essentially a feeding migration and they grow quickly on a diet of shrimps, sand eels, young herrings, sprats and capelin, returning 1-4 years later to spawn. The migration can take them up to the Norwegian Sea and across to Greenland, navigating by the sun and the stars, until they return to the vicinity of their home river and detect the stream of their birth by smell. Almost all salmon return to their home stream to spawn.

53

Trout

TROUT
Salmo trutta

1·4 m (sea trout), 1 m (brown trout). Streamlined body with a pointed head, body compressed from side to side and deepest at origin of dorsal fin. Long upper jaw bone extends well past the level of the rear of the eye. Body deep in front of tail fin, with fin rays merging gently into outline of tail. Body scales small, 13-16 rows between base of adipose fin and lateral line. 14-17 short, stubby gill rakers on the first arch. Coloration very variable. Sea trout silvery with black and reddish spots — some of which are always present on the gill covers. Brown trout darker, greeny-brown on the back with numerous black and red spots; very few spots on tail and dorsal fins. Young trout have a line of dark smudges on their sides and are heavily spotted with orange and black; rear edge of adipose fin orange.

Distribution: across Europe from Ireland eastwards to the Caspian Sea, and from northern Norway to Spain and the tip of North Africa. Confined to rivers and lakes in the south of its range; also found in the sea from northern Spain northwards, across to Iceland.

Natural history: the trout exists in

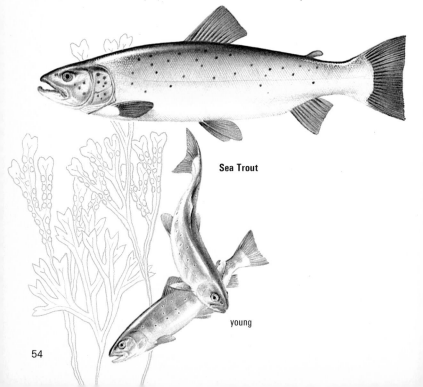

Sea Trout

young

several biological forms which are sometimes described as subspecies. The brown trout lives in fresh water and is heavily coloured and usually rather small, though size is often affected by the amount of food available and the size of the river or lake. Rather larger fish, silvery in colour but with heavy spots, live in large lakes and big rivers and in the north of its range occur the sea trout, which migrate to the sea to feed. All spawn in fresh water October-January, the eggs being laid in a shallow nest made by the female in gravel beds in the river. The eggs hatch in 6-8 weeks, and the fry live in the gravel for a further 4-6 weeks before beginning to feed on small crustaceans. Later they eat insect larvae as well, and flying insects at the surface, while the large lake trout and sea trout eat fishes.

RAINBOW TROUT
Salmo gairdneri
1 m. Body similar to the brown trout but very variable in form and colouring due

These young fish show the black smudges (parr marks) on the sides typical of young salmon family fishes.

to selective breeding (in Europe) and different races. Scales small, 15-16 in a row between adipose fin and lateral line. 16-22 medium-sized gill rakers on the first arch. Coloration is best distinguishing feature; the back and sides have numerous black spots which extend onto the dorsal and tail fins.

Distribution: native along the Pacific coast of North America from north Mexico to Alaska, now widespread in Europe, mostly as result of introduction on trout farms.

Natural history: breeds October-March, the eggs being laid in gravel nests in river beds. They hatch in 14-21 weeks and, after a period in the gravel, the young fish spread out through the rivers. Most European stocks are raised in hatcheries, where the eggs are collected and fertilized in artificial conditions.

Rainbow Trout

CHARR
Salvelinus alpinus
1 m (migratory form), 25 cm (lake form). Body similar in shape to the trout except that the body between the adipose fin and the tail is narrow. Upper jaw bone reaches to the level of the rear edge of the eye or just beyond. Teeth in the roof of the mouth in a patch at the front not in a staggered line down the middle of the palate. Scales minute, 123-153 in lateral line. Front edges of pectoral, pelvic and anal fins all light.
Distribution: from middle Norway and Iceland northwards occurs in the sea and migrates to spawn in rivers, ranging around the whole of the Arctic ice cap. Also found in numerous lakes in the British Isles, Scandinavia, Germany, and in mountainous areas of Switzerland.

Natural history: like the salmon and the trout, the charr occurs in several forms: most notably as a large migratory form which goes to the sea to feed and spawns in rivers, and as much smaller forms in landlocked lakes. Many of these were once regarded as distinct species, but it is now generally recognized that they represent a single species complex. However it has recently been suggested that there are two species complexes involved. In lakes, charr spawn in winter or spring usually in fairly deep water; in rivers they spawn on gravel bottom shallows. The eggs and young fish are covered by ice through the winter and the young only become active when the ice clears in spring. In lakes charr feed mainly on small crustaceans, but also eat insect larvae, molluscs and even small fishes.

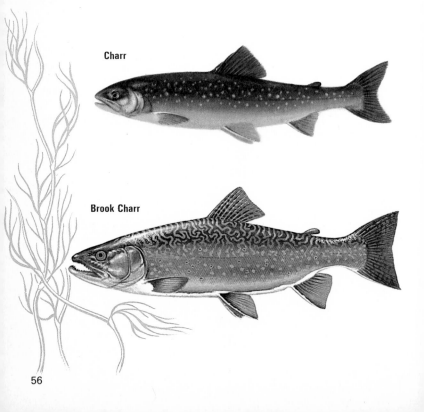

Charr

Brook Charr

Humpback Salmon

The migratory forms, which eat crustaceans and fishes when they are in the sea, grow to a larger size than lake forms. Many of the isolated lake populations are threatened with extinction by the introduction of predators and competitors, the adaption of lakes for hydro-electric schemes and by acid rainfall.

BROOK CHARR
Salvelinus fontinalis
50 cm. Similar to the Arctic charr with very small scales on the body (110-130 in lateral line). Upper jaw bone reaches past eye edge. 14-22 gill rakers on the first gill arch. Coloration distinctive but variable in detail; front edges of anal, pelvic and pectoral fins white with a black band behind, back greenish-brown with wavy creamy lines all over, creamy spots on sides.
Distribution: native to eastern North America from Cape Cod to northern Canada and westwards to the Great Lakes and the Mississippi. Introduced widely into Europe; still mostly bred in farms, where it is stocked for its strong fighting qualities, as well as its fine flavour. It is sometimes deliberately crossed with brown or rainbow trout.

Natural history: breeds in gravel in running water October-March, the eggs hatch in spring when the young disperse into shallow nursery areas where they live for up to 2 years before moving into deeper water and larger rivers. They feed on insects, insect larvae, crustaceans and small fishes.

HUMPBACK SALMON
Oncorhynchus gorbuscha
64 cm. Similar to Atlantic salmon, but with long upper jaw bone extending beyond rear edge of eye. Immediately distinguished by the long-based anal fin with 13-19 full-length rays. Scales very small, 147-205 in lateral line. Spawning males develop a strong hump on the back and turn a deep red colour.
Distribution: native to the North Pacific Ocean from California to Canada, and the Siberian coast. Introduced to the north coast of the USSR (White Sea) and subsequently found in Norwegian, Icelandic and British rivers.
Natural history: breeds September-October in nests made in gravel in rivers. Eggs hatch in 14-17 weeks, depending on river temperature. Young move downstream in their first summer then to the sea, returning in 2-3 years to breed They eat small crustaceans and insect larvae, but once in the sea feed on crustaceans and fishes. Humpback salmon traverse the North Pacific on their migrations. Known as pink salmon, they are an important food fish, hence their introduction into European rivers.

ADRIATIC SALMON
Salmothymus obtusirostris
50 cm. A typical member of the salmon family, distinguished from the trout by its short blunt snout, and rather large upper jaw bone reaching just beyond the eye. Body scales moderately large, 101-103 scales in lateral line.
Distribution: occurs only in streams in Dalmatia – part of the Adriatic coast of Yugoslavia.
Natural history: breeds in streams October-December, laying eggs in gravel in a shallow nest hollowed by the female. Feeds on crustaceans and insect larvae, and occasionally eats fishes when older. Non-migratory, this fish lives all its life in streams and the lakes into which they flow. Little-known, it is probably a descendant of the salmon which lived in the Mediter-ranean soon after the Ice Ages.

HUCHEN
Hucho huchc
120 cm. Salmon-like in general appear-ance, although rather narrow-bodied and with a large head. Long upper jawbone reaches well past the rear of the eye. Scales very small, 180-200 in lateral line. Coloration, greenish on the back, sides silvery with numerous dark x-shaped spots.

Adriatic Salmon

Distribution: lives only in the River Danube and its larger tributaries. Attempted introductions to the Thames, Rhine and Elbe failed.
Natural history: mainly confined to the middle and upper reaches of the Danube. Spawning takes place on gravel beds in fast-flowing sections of the stream in spring (usually mid-April). The young live in the small rivers, feeding on crustaceans and small fishes, but grow quickly and spread out into the larger river within a year. Adults feed mostly on fishes, especially *Chon-drostoma nasus*. The huchen has be-come very restricted in its range due to dams and pollution in the Danube.

Huchen

SMELT FAMILY
Osmeridae

The smelts are a small family comprising some 10 species worldwide. Most are marine fishes found in coastal and inshore waters but some are abundant in estuaries and other low salinity areas and the true smelts spawn in fresh water. The family is confined to the Arctic Ocean and the northern parts of the Atlantic and Pacific Oceans – being most abundant in the latter. They are all relatively small fishes and usually occur in enormous schools. Several species are exploited commercially by man, and they are all important in the food chains of the sea and fresh water in which they live, either as prey for larger animals or as predators on smaller animals. The smelts all have a fleshy, rayless adipose fin on the back.

SMELT
Osmerus eperlanus
30 cm. Slender but round-bodied, with a pointed head and prominent lower jaw. Dorsal fin short-based; anal fin long with 12-16 rays; adipose fin prominent. The large mouth has strong curved teeth in the jaws, on the tongue and in the palate. When fresh, has a strong smell of cucumber.

Distribution: coastal waters, estuaries, rivers and lakes of Europe, from northern France and the British Isles northwards to the White Sea. Abundant in the Baltic.

Natural history: most smelt live in coastal waters and estuaries and spawn in fresh water in rivers, but some populations live in lakes which have been landlocked since the last Ice Age. They spawn in early spring in rivers over sand or gravel, and over submerged plants, but many eggs break away and develop suspended by their parachute-like outer covering in the tidal water. Eggs hatch in 1-4 weeks, according to temperature. At all ages smelts eat crustaceans, but adults eat large numbers of small fishes, especially young sprat, herring and whiting. Adults return to the sea after spawning; young fish stay in the river and move down to the sea in autumn. The smelt is now rare in many rivers due to pollution.

Smelt

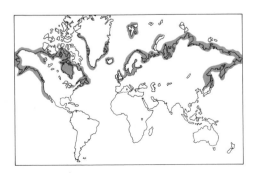

The smelt family are marine and coastal freshwater fishes, often migratory. Most numerous species occur in North America and the North Pacific basin.

59

CARP FAMILY
Cyprinidae

The carp family is the dominant family of freshwater fishes in Europe, North America, Africa and Asia. It is not found at all in Australia, nor in South America – whose fresh waters are dominated by characins, like the tetras and piranhas, and catfishes. With around 270 genera and 1,600 species, it is the largest known family of fishes. The species of the carp family are typically 'fish-shaped', with scaly bodies, a single dorsal fin, no adipose fin, and often with barbels around the mouth. They all have scaleless heads and toothless mouths, and all lack a stomach – the gut being undifferentiated from throat to vent. Another internal feature, which is of great significance to their life style, is the modification of the first four vertebrae to provide a series of movable bones linking the inner ear to the swimbladder, which is very well developed. This results in their being able to hear sounds transmitted through water exceptionally well. Members of this family also have the ability to detect very minute amounts of 'alarm substance' released from the skin of an injured fish of the same species. These two features are both extremely useful to fishes which live mainly in the rather coloured waters of inland lakes and rivers where plant growth and sediment in the water reduces visibility. These conditions are also reflected in the well-developed barbels of many cyprinid fishes, particularly the bottom-living species, for the barbels are highly sensitive organs of taste and play an important role in food detection.

At spawning time, the adults of the carp family develop hard, white, conical outgrowths on the skin of the head, the front parts of the body and the pectoral fins. These contact organs, particularly well-developed in the males, are believed to play a role in species- and sex-recognition at spawning time. Despite this, however, it is not uncommon to find naturally occurring hybrids between species – and even genera – in Europe's fresh waters. But these hybrids, which share the features of both parents, are usually not able to reproduce themselves, and are often very difficult to identify.

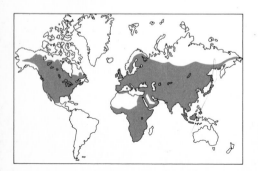

Right: the carp, which gives the family its name, shows many typical features: barbels round the mouth, scaleless head, scaly body, and a single fin on the back.
An entirely freshwater family, it is very rare to find any of its members even in brackish waters. With about 1,600 species, it is the largest known fish family.

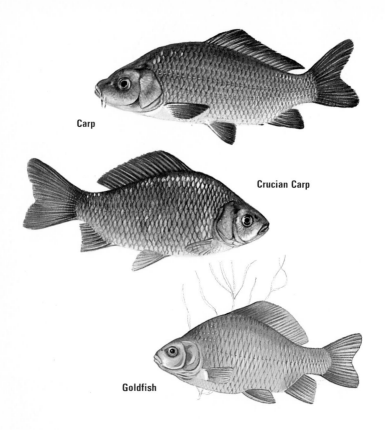

Carp

Crucian Carp

Goldfish

CARP
Cyprinus carpio
1·02 m. Deep-bodied, usually covered with large scales (except for the artificial breeds: leather carp with no scales and mirror carp with a few large scales). All have two pairs of barbels, those in the angle of the mouth are larger. Dorsal fin concave in outline, long-based with 17-22 branched rays, and a strong toothed spine in front.
Distribution: native to the River Danube and the rivers of the Black Sea basin, now introduced throughout Europe (except for the far north) and many other parts of the world.
Natural history: thrives in lakes and lowland rivers where the flow is slow, the water warm, and there are abundant

water plants. Carp feed on bottom-living insect larvae, snails, crustaceans and plants. They feed mainly at night or in twilight conditions, but at low temperatures eat very little. Breeding takes place in late spring among dense plant growth in shallow water, the eggs being attached to the plants. The eggs, small (1-1·5 mm) and very numerous, hatch in 3-8 days depending on temperature. As the carp has been introduced to much of Europe, its success depends very largely on local conditions. Much of northern Europe and most of the British Isles are too cold for it, and as a result it breeds successfully only in the warmest of years. It may live for 20-30 years.

CRUCIAN CARP
Carassius carassius
51 cm. Very deep-bodied, with a relatively small head. Scales moderately large, 31-36 in lateral line. No barbels around mouth. Dorsal fin convex in outline, moderately long-based, with 14-21 branched rays, and a lightly toothed spine in front. 26-31 gill rakers on the first gill arch.
Distribution: widely distributed in Europe, except for parts of Spain, Italy, Greece and Norway. Only in eastern England.
Natural history: an inhabitant of marshy pools, overgrown lakes and the backwaters of slow-flowing lowland rivers, in which it survives due to its ability to tolerate low oxygen levels and cold winters. Breeds in late spring in shallow weedy areas, the deep golden eggs, attached to water plants, hatching in 5-7 days. The young fish hang on the plant leaves for 2-3 days after hatching while they use up the yolk of the egg. The food of the crucian carp is mainly insect larvae, particularly midge larvae, water snails and crustaceans, but it also eats large quantities of plants. Growth and body form are strongly dependent on available food; if food is scarce the fish grow slowly.

GOLDFISH
Carassius auratus auratus
30 cm. Body moderately deep with a rather large head. Scales fairly large, 27-31 in the lateral line. Dorsal fin long-based with 15-19 branched rays and a deeply-serrated spine in front of these rays; the outline of the fin is straight to slightly concave. 35-48 gill rakers on the first gill arch. Greeny-brown on the back with bronze sides when young; orange-red when adult.
Distribution: native to China and parts of Siberia, the goldfish has been introduced throughout southern and middle Europe.
Natural history: lives in small lakes and the backwaters of slow-flowing lowland rivers. Breeds among water plants in summer, when the temperature reaches 20°C, the eggs being attached to plant leaves. Breeding in natural waters in northern Europe is infrequent because of the cold, but in southern Europe the goldfish breeds prolifically.

Originally native to China, the goldfish was introduced as a pond fish but now lives wild in parts of Europe.

GIBEL CARP
Carassius auratus gibelio
36 cm. Body moderately deep but with a rather small head. Medium-sized scales, 28-32 in lateral line. Dorsal fin long-based with 15-18 branched rays and a deeply serrated spine in front; the outline of the fin is straight. 39-50 gill rakers on first gill arch. Greeny-brown on the back with golden-green sides in both young and adult fishes.
Distribution: native to western Siberia and eastwards to Europe, including the Baltic and Black Sea basins.
Natural history: this is the European subspecies of the goldfish to which its natural history is virtually identical. Due to the introduction of the Asiatic subspecies it is now very difficult to be certain of the original range of the western form.

DACE
Leuciscus leuciscus
30 cm. A slender-bodied silvery fish, with a narrow, rather pointed head and a small mouth. Short-based dorsal fin, placed directly over the pelvic fins, has 7-8 full length branched rays. The anal fin is short-based with 8-9 branched rays. Outer margin of both fins concave. Scales quite small; 48-51 in lateral line.
Distribution: throughout Europe, north of the Pyrenees and Alps, but not in Norway or northern USSR. Absent in Ireland (except where introduced in the south), and in Scotland.
Natural history: a fish of clear, flowing water, especially common in small rivers and streams. It also occurs in lakes though not in large numbers and usually only as an accidental introduction (during floods or by man). Lives in large schools in mid-water or at the surface. Dace usually spawn at night in shallow gravelly areas – generally in April though sometimes as early as February or as late as May, depending on local climate and water temperature. The pale orange eggs measure 1·5 mm in diameter and are shed in the gravel in which they develop for three weeks at 13°C. The young are 7·5 mm when they hatch and grow rapidly; maturing at the end of their second year. Few dace live longer than 7 years. When young their food consists mainly of diatoms and small crustaceans but they soon begin taking small insects at the surface and insect larvae. They feed heavily on insects, particularly flying insects at the surface of the river, but also eat a considerable amount of plant food including both algae and higher plants.

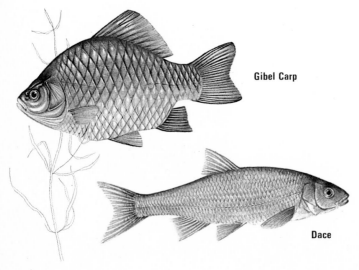

Gibel Carp

Dace

CHUB
Leuciscus cephalus
61 cm. Slender-bodied and silvery, broad across back and head; with a blunt head and large mouth. Both dorsal and anal fins are high but short-based; dorsal has 8-9 branched rays and is level with the rear end of the pelvic fin base; anal fin has 7-9 branched rays. The free edges of both are convex. Scales are moderately large, 44-46 in the lateral line.

Distribution: throughout Europe except for Ireland, northern Scotland and northern Scandinavia.

Natural history: a river fish found most abundantly in moderately large rivers with a fairly slow current, but also occurs in numbers in fast-flowing streams which have deep, slow-flowing pools. It also lives in lakes in which the water is of good quality with high dissolved oxygen levels. Spawns May-June in shallow water close to water plants, often in small tributary streams. Eggs hatch in 8-10 days. Chub live for 10-12 years, some even to 25 years. Feeds on a wide range of insect larvae and crustaceans, and large chub eat fishes, frogs and occasionally water voles.

IDE
Leuciscus idus
1 m. Slender-bodied and silvery, but with a broad head and a rather curved back; the snout is blunt and the mouth oblique. Dorsal fin has 8 branched rays and originates behind pelvic fin base; the anal fin, with 9-10 rays, is concave on its free edge. Scales are small, 56-61 in lateral line. Back greenish-brown, sides silvery with reddish pelvic and anal fins. The ornamental golden orfe, which is the same species, is deep orange.

Distribution: native to the Danube basin and northern Europe except for Norway. Introduced to parts of Britain and France. Absent southern Europe.

Natural history: inhabits the lower reaches of large rivers, lakes in their flood plain, and brackish areas, especially of the Baltic. Lives in deep water in schools, coming into shallower fresh water to spawn among weeds and gravel April-May. The eggs adhere to plant leaves and hatch in 15-20 days. The young feed on small planktonic crustaceans, larger ide eat insect larvae, crustaceans and molluscs, and big specimens eat fishes. An important food fish in parts of inland Europe.

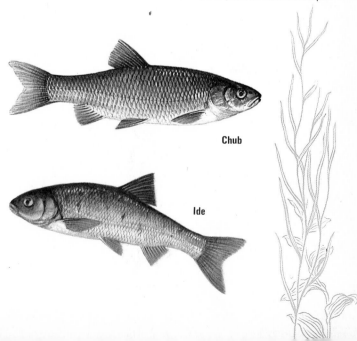

Chub

Ide

SOUFFIE
Leuciscus souffia
20 cm. Slender-bodied with a small, pointed head. Both dorsal and anal fins short-based with sinuous or slightly convex free edges; anal fin has 8-9 branched rays. Scales moderate in size, 45-48 in lateral line. Wide dark stripe along the sides; the lateral line picked out in orange.

Distribution: lives in southern France and northern Italy, and in the upper Rhine and the Danube.

Natural history: a schooling fish living in the upper reaches of rivers and some highland lakes. Feeds on insects, crustaceans and algae. Spawns April-July in shallow, flowing water over gravel beds, laying 5,500-8,000 eggs. Both sexes develop white tubercles on the head and body before spawning.

MODERLIESCHEN
Leucaspius delineatus
12 cm. A slender silvery fish with large, thin and very easily detached scales; the body compressed, with flattened sides and a sharp keel between the pelvic fins and the vent. Anal fin long-based with 10-13 branched rays. Lateral line pores on only the first 8-10 scales. Mouth strongly oblique.

Distribution: central and eastern Europe, northwards to southern Sweden; absent from Britain, France, Spain, Portugal, Italy and the Adriatic countries.

Natural history: lives in large schools in lowland lakes and slow-flowing rivers which have become overgrown with vegetation. Can tolerate high temperatures and low oxygen levels. Spawns June-July, the eggs being looped around plants in strips. The female has a short egg-laying tube from her vent; the male guards the eggs. Feeds mainly on insect larvae taken near the surface, and crustaceans.

ROACH
Rutilus rutilus
53 cm. Body elongate, but becomes deeper with age. Head small; mouth relatively small and terminal, no barbels. The short-based dorsal fin, originating above the base of the pelvic fins, has 9-10 branched rays. The longer-based anal fin has 9-11 branched rays. Scales are large, 42-45 in lateral line. The iris of the eye is red. Back bluish or greeny-brown, sides intensely silvery but in large fish yellowish to bronze. Pelvic and anal fins orange to deep red; pectoral and tail fins reddish, but upper tail fin and dorsal dark.

Distribution: widespread in Europe except the Iberian and Italian peninsulas, Greece, Norway and Scotland. Introduced to southern Scotland, Wales and Ireland.

Natural history: a highly adaptable fish which lives in lowland rivers and lakes, preferring slow currents in the former but also found in fast-flowing

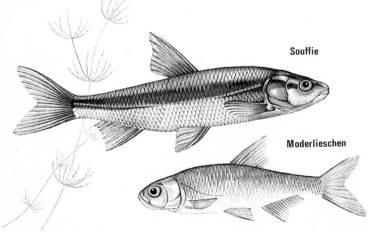

Souffie

Moderlieschen

Roach

streams. Tolerates both high and low temperatures and survives in moderately low oxygen levels. As a result has spread throughout Europe, in canals and man-made still waters such as gravel pits and reservoirs. Also tolerates brackish water and is common in low-salinity areas of the Baltic. Spawns April-June in schools, shedding its eggs among water plants in shallow water. The yellow eggs, 1-1·5 mm in diameter, stick to the leaves; 1,000-15,000 eggs are laid per female depending on her size. They hatch in 9-12 days at 12-14°C, and after a further day or two on the vegetation, the larvae become mobile and soon form large schools in shallow water. These small fishes eat diatoms and small crustaceans, but soon move to a wide ranging diet of whatever invertebrates are most common. Insect larvae, crustaceans, worms and molluscs are their main diet; they also eat large quantities of plant matter. Growth is greatly affected by the amount of available food, and in water where predators are scarce roach will quickly become overcrowded and stunted. In good conditions they will live for up to 12 years, becoming sexually mature at 2-3 years of age. An important food fish in inland Europe; in the British Isles it is mainly regarded as an angler's fish.

The roach is one of Europe's commonest and most widespread fish. Forming a school is a means of protecting themselves from predators.

DANUBIAN ROACH
Rutilus pigus
40 cm. A rather slender fish with a small head and silvery scales. Very similar to the roach but has smaller and more numerous scales, 45-49 in lateral line. Dorsal fin high and short-based, with 10-11 branched rays; anal fin longer-based with 10-13 rays. The pelvic, anal and lower caudal fins are reddish; the other fins dark olive. The body has an iridescent sheen on the sides. The lining of the body cavity is dark.

Distribution: lives in the large lakes and rivers of northern Italy and in the Danube's middle and upper reaches.

Natural history: an inhabitant of slow-flowing rivers and lakes in which it lives in rather deep water. Spawns April-May among weeds in moderately shallow water, laying 35,000-60,000 eggs per female according to size. Feeds on worms, molluscs and crustaceans, and considerable quantities of plant matter. The northern Italian populations are regarded as a separate subspecies, *Rutilus pigus pigus*, from the Danubian populations which are known as *Rutilus pigus virgo*.

ADRIATIC ROACH
Rutilus rubilio
30 cm. A slender fish with a small head; mouth small and terminal. Scales moderately large, 36-44 in lateral line. Dorsal fin placed above the base of the pelvics, high but short-based with 8-9 branched rays. Anal fin long-based with 8-10 branched rays. Back olive brown; sides silvery white, with a scale-wide grey to blackish band running from eye to tail. Pelvic and anal fins reddish; other fins grey green.

Distribution: in Italy (although absent from some southern rivers), Yugoslavia, Albania and Greece.

Natural history: occurs mainly in slow-flowing rivers and lakes where vegetation is abundant. A hardy species which can survive even in hot spring water with temperatures of 25-27°C. Feeds on a wide range of invertebrates, chiefly insects and crustaceans, but also eats quantities of algae and plants. Breeds March-June, spawning in schools in shallow water among vegetation; the eggs are small, 1-1·5 mm in diameter.

CALANDINO ROACH
Rutilus alburnoides
20 cm. A slender-bodied fish with a small head (about one quarter the length of the body without the tail fin). The profile of the head and back is nearly straight, then falls in a smooth curve from the dorsal fin to the very narrow tail. Scales rather large, 39-40 in lateral line. Dorsal fin short-based, with 7 branched rays and a convex edge; anal fin rather longer-based, with 7-9 rays and a straight edge. Back and upper sides green with silvery reflections, flanks silvery; a narrow diffuse black band between the head and the tail fin. Pelvic and anal fins reddish.

Distribution: occurs only in the rivers of Portugal and southern Spain.

Natural history: lives in schools in lowland rivers and lakes. Breeds April-May among aquatic plants and on stony bottoms in shallow water. Feeds on invertebrates, chiefly small crustaceans and insect larvae. The natural history and relationships of this small fish are very poorly known.

PEARL ROACH
Rutilus frisii
60 cm. A long-bodied but robust fish, cylindrical in cross-section; head small, snout bluntly rounded, mouth small and terminal. Dorsal fin short-based but high, with 11-12 branched rays; anal fin longer-based, high, with 12-14 branched rays. Scales numerous and small, 62-67 in lateral line. Colouring greeny-brown on the back, sides silvery; fins greyish, the pelvic and anal fins touched with red. At spawning time large, white contact organs on head and body look like pearls.

Distribution: rivers on the northern coast of the Black Sea *(Rutilus frisii frisii)* and in lakes at the head of the Danube river *(Rutilus frisii meidingeri)*.

Natural history: the Danubian subspecies, confined to lakes, is now seriously threatened with extinction. It lives in small schools in deep water, but spawns in shallow water in the tributaries feeding the lakes in April-May. The eggs, laid among weed and over gravel, hatch in about 10 days. Becomes sexually mature at 3-5 years and may live as long as 12 years.

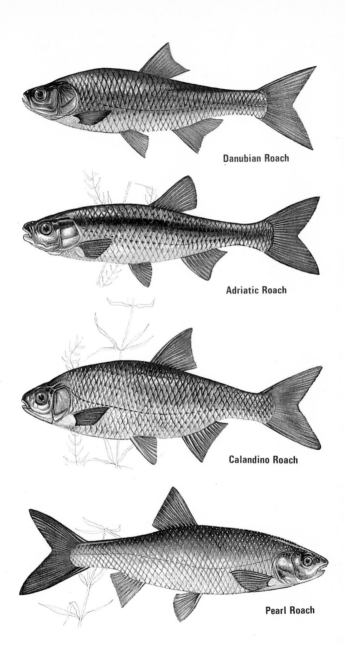

Danubian Roach

Adriatic Roach

Calandino Roach

Pearl Roach

Rudd

RUDD
Scardinius erythrophthalmus
45 cm. A deep-bodied fish with a small head and a medium-sized, steeply angled mouth. Dorsal fin, originating well behind level of pelvic fin base, is high with 8-9 branched rays; anal fin long-based with 10-11 branched rays. Scales medium-sized, 40-45 in lateral line. Sharp keel on belly between pelvic fins and vent. Deep greeny brown on back, silvery on sides (bronze in large fish); all fins with a reddish tinge but the pelvics and anal scarlet.
Distribution: widespread across Europe north of the Pyrenees; absent from Scotland, Norway and northern Finland and Sweden.
Natural history: the rudd is typically an inhabitant of lakes and backwaters of rivers; but is uncommon in the main stream of the river. Thrives in still waters or man-made pools such as marl pits, gravel workings and peat cuttings, but only when the water has matured and grown dense vegetation. Rudd assemble in large schools often swimming near the surface where they feed on surface insects and their larvae; they also eat crustaceans and certain underwater plants. They spawn April-June among water plants and in reed-beds. The eggs stick to the leaves and hatch in 8-15 days depending on the temperature. Between 90,000-200,000 eggs are laid by each female.

GREEK RUDD
Scardinius graecus
40 cm. A shallow-bodied fish with a small head and medium-sized, steeply angled mouth. The profile of the head is concave; that of the back convex to the beginning of the dorsal fin. The maximum depth of the body is about level with the pectoral fin. Dorsal fin high, 9-10 branched rays; anal fin longer-based, 10-12 branched rays.
Distribution: occurs only in the southern tip of the Greek mainland.
Natural history: the Greek rudd lives in lakes and slow-flowing rivers forming large schools. Spawns April-June among underwater plants in shallow water. Feeds on small crustaceans, the larvae and pupae of insects, and on plant material. The majority of its food is taken at or near the surface and the fish is not usually found in deep water. Very little is known about the biology of this species, though it is important locally, both to anglers and as a commercial species.

Right: the deep scarlet fins of the rudd set it apart from most of its relatives. Although it looks brightly coloured with shiny sides, its coloration is not at all obvious in the peaty water in which it lives.

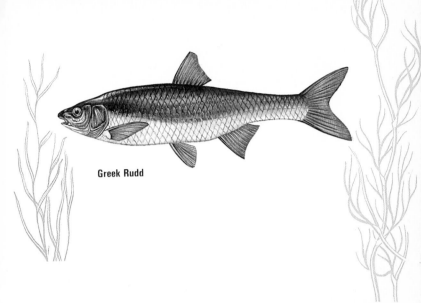

Greek Rudd

Bitterling
female

BITTERLING
Rhodeus sericeus

9 cm. A deep-bodied little fish, with flattened sides but giving the impression of plumpness. Head relatively small, eye large, mouth terminal but slightly oblique. Scales large and firmly attached, about 35 along the sides, and a row of only 5 or 6 with lateral line pores above the pectoral fin. Dorsal fin long-based, convex in outline, with 8-9 branched rays; anal fin shorter, also convex, with 7-8 branched rays. Both sexes have an iridescent stripe along the sides of the tail; the sides are silvery with a pinkish flush. When spawning the pink colour of the male becomes very pronounced as do the white contact tubercles on the head.

Distribution: throughout Europe except for the Iberian Peninsula, southern France, Italy, the Balkans, and northern Finland and Sweden. Absent from Ireland and Scotland but introduced to England.

Natural history: an inhabitant of slow-flowing rivers and river backwaters, lakes, and ponds in lowland areas, favouring places with dense aquatic vegetation. Breeds April-June,

The breeding behaviour of the bitterling is unique in Europe. Here the pair inspect a freshwater mussel in which the eggs will be laid; the female has a long egg-laying tube from her vent.

when the male develops his bright breeding colours and contact tubercles and the female a long egg-laying tube from the vent. The eggs are laid within the gill chamber of the freshwater swan mussel, a bottom-living inhabitant of still or slow-flowing waters, and the male fertilizes them by ejecting sperm into the mussel's inhalent breathing tube. The eggs, which are fairly large (3 mm) and relatively few (10-25 each mussel), hatch in 3-4 weeks. The larva has a horny process on the yolk sac which lodges in the mussel's gills. Young fish leave the mussel a few days after hatching. The success of such a nest is reflected in the few eggs the bitterling lays, at most 100 per female annually. The young mature in 2-3 years; few live as long as 5 years. The bitterling is frequently the host for the mussel's parasitic larvae which cling to the fish's fin rays and are carried away from their parent, ensuring a wide distribution for the mollusc. Bitterling feed on small invertebrates, especially planktonic crustaceans and small insect larvae. They also eat plant matter, mainly filamentous and encrusting algae and some higher plants.

SPANISH MINNOWCARP
Pseudophoxinus hispanicus
7·5 cm. A small, slender fish, with a relatively small head and a strongly oblique mouth. Dorsal fin, originating behind the level of the pelvic fins, is short-based with 7 branched rays. Anal fin similar, with 8 branched rays. Scales relatively small; 62-68 in lateral line. Back grey-green, upper sides golden and belly silvery; a narrow dark stripe runs the length of the fish, becoming more intense towards the tail.

Distribution: lives only in rivers in southern Portugal and central southern Spain.

Natural history: forms schools in rivers and streams. Spawns in late spring, and feeds on small invertebrates. The biology of this interesting endemic species is virtually unknown. Often placed in the genus *Phoxinellus*, its nearest relatives appear to be the bleaks, but even its generic name is doubtful.

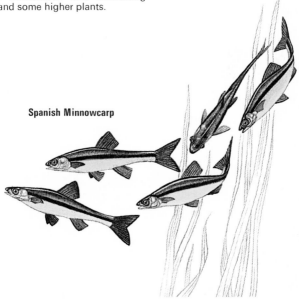

Spanish Minnowcarp

MINNOW
Phoxinus phoxinus
12 cm. A small, slender-bodied fish which is round in cross-section. Both dorsal and anal fins short-based and rounded, the dorsal with 7 branched rays, the anal with 6-7 branched rays. Head rather small and blunt, mouth oblique. Body covered with minute scales, lateral line interrupted towards tail. Colour variable usually greeny-brown above, with golden sides and a white belly. A line of dark blotches runs along the sides. At spawning time the males have bright red bellies and con-spicuous white contact organs.

Distribution: across Europe from Ireland, where it has been introduced, to the USSR. Absent from Norway, most of Spain, Italy and Greece.

Natural history: a common fish in the upper reaches of rivers preferring clean running water. Also occurs in large lowland rivers and large lakes. Forms huge schools in shallow water often near the surface and is a very active fish. Moves into deeper water in winter, taking shelter in small groups under bankside vegetation or behind rocks in the river bed. Spawns in late spring (May-July) over gravel stretches to which the eggs adhere. They hatch in 5-10 days and become sexually mature in 2-3 years. Each female lays 200-1,000 eggs. The minnow feeds on insect larvae, crustaceans and plants, but in summer also eats flying insects.

SWAMP MINNOW
Phoxinus percnurus
18 m. A small, minnow-like fish with a rather deeper, less rounded body than a minnow. Dorsal and anal fins rounded and short-based, with 9 branched rays in the dorsal and 8-9 in the anal. Head medium-sized, snout blunt and mouth terminal. Scales minute, 68-97 in lateral line.

Distribution: central Europe, across northern Poland and the USSR.

Natural history: lives in lakes, ponds, and stagnant backwaters of rivers where the water is shallow and often choked with vegetation. Spawns on the leaves of water plants to which its eggs are attached. Eggs hatch in 5-8 days; from 1,600-18,000 eggs are laid by each female. Feeds on insect larvae, crustaceans and flying insects at the water's surface.

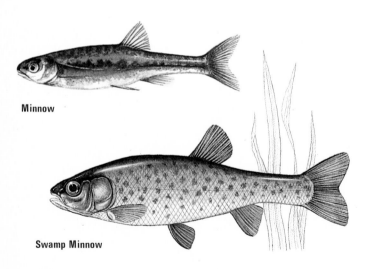

Minnow

Swamp Minnow

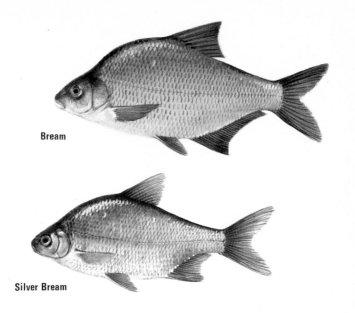

Bream

Silver Bream

BREAM
Abramis brama
80 cm. A massive, deep-bodied fish with flat sides and a high back. Dorsal fin short-based and high; 9 branched rays. Anal fin long-based, higher in front than at midway; 24-30 branched rays. Scales small, 51-60 in lateral line. Body exceptionally slimy. Eye small.

Distribution: widely distributed across Europe, but absent from the Iberian and Italian peninsulas, the Balkans, Norway and north Scotland.

Natural history: a fish of slow-flowing lowland rivers, lakes, reservoirs; occurs in brackish water in the Baltic but breeds in fresh water. Forms schools when swimming actively in mid-water and when feeding on the bottom. Adopts an oblique head-down posture to feed, its tubular mouth to the bottom to detect food buried in the mud, puffing the mud away with mouthfuls of water until the food is exposed. Eats worms, molluscs, insect larvae and crustaceans. Breeds May-June among dense plants in shallow water. The yellowish eggs stick to the plants, hatching in 3-12 days.

SILVER BREAM
Blicca bjoerkna
36 cm. Deep-bodied and flat-sided like the bream, with steep dorsal profile from head to fin. Head small, snout blunt with a slightly oblique terminal mouth. Eye large; equal in diameter to snout length. Dorsal fin high, short-based; 11 branched rays; anal fin long, but less so than the bream, with 21-23 branched rays. Always silvery in colour.

Distribution: across Europe from eastern England to the USSR. Absent from Norway, northern Sweden, southern France, the Iberian and Italian peninsulas.

Natural history: lives in the lower reaches of rivers where the flow is slow; also adapts to still waters and is very common in reservoirs. Feeds in mid-water on bottom-eating insect larvae, crustaceans, small molluscs and some plant material. Breeds in June in schools among plants, the yellow eggs sticking to the leaves and hatching in 4-6 days at a length of 4·8 mm. Males arrive at the spawning grounds first, and the female lays several batches of eggs during the season.

DANUBE BREAM
Abramis sapa
30 cm. Similar to the bream but the body not so high; strongly flattened at the sides. Head small, snout blunt, with a rather small sub-terminal mouth. Dorsal fin short-based and high, 11 branched rays. Anal fin very long, the front rays only slightly longer than those midway; 36-41 branched rays. Scales moderately large; 48-52 in lateral line. Eye relatively large.
Distribution: found in the middle and lower reaches of the River Danube and the rivers running into the northern Black and Caspian Seas.
Natural history: a schooling fish of large deep lowland rivers, and estuaries

The bream's down-turned mouth, typical of a bottom-feeding fish, can be protruded into a tube. The long anal fin tends to keep the fish's head tilted down as it swims.

where the water is brackish. The populations in such areas migrate to fresh water to spawn. Spawns April-May on the river bed in running water, the bottom being clear of mud or sediment. Sexually mature in 4 years, it grows slowly but rarely lives longer than 8 years. 8,000-150,000 eggs are laid per female. Feeds exclusively on bottom-living invertebrates, mainly insect larvae and snails but also crustaceans and worms.

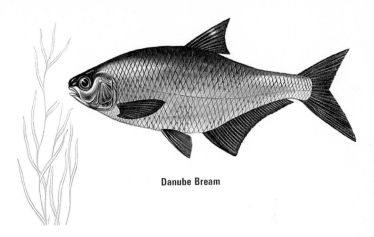

Danube Bream

BLUE BREAM
Abramis ballerus
41 cm. Similar to the bream, its body deep and even more laterally compressed. Head small, eye moderately large, mouth slightly oblique and terminal. Dorsal fin short-based and very high; 11-12 branched rays. Anal fin higher in front than elsewhere, very long-based; 38-48 branched rays. Scales small; 66-73 in lateral line. Back blue grey; sides silvery with a yellowish flush.
Distribution: River Danube and major rivers of the northern Black Sea, also the rivers of the south and central Baltic Sea including Sweden.

Natural history: lives in rivers in the lowlands and in lakes and reservoirs. Forms schools in shallows for the first two years of its life; in open water when adult. Feeds mainly near the surface on planktonic crustaceans. Breeds April-June in places where there is both underwater vegetation and clean gravel exposed. 4,000-25,000 eggs are produced per female. Sexually mature in 3-4 years.

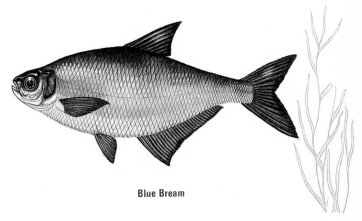

Blue Bream

77

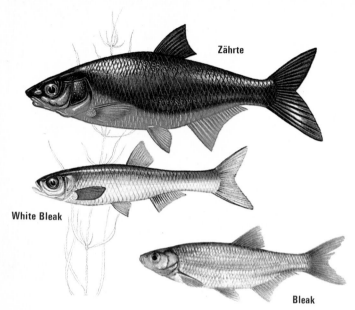

Zährte

White Bleak

Bleak

ZÄHRTE
Vimba vimba
50 cm. Moderately deep-bodied, with a fairly high back and flattened sides. Head small with a blunt but projecting fleshy snout, always longer than the eye; mouth inferior with thick horse-shoe shaped lips. Scales small; 51-64 in lateral line. A scaleless keel between pelvic and anal fin bases; a scaled keel behind the dorsal fin. Dorsal fin short-based, moderately high, 10-11 branched rays; anal fin long, high in front, 18-21 branched rays. In breeding season the back is black, with orange patches on the gill covers and the bases of the pelvic and anal fins.
Distribution: from the Elbe and Danube rivers eastwards to the Caspian basin. Present in southern Sweden and Finland.
Natural history: occurs in the middle and lower reaches of rivers, even in low salinity areas in the Baltic. Schools move up river to spawn May-July, often migrating long distances. Spawns on a clean stony bottom free from mud and silt, laying its eggs in several spawnings. Eggs hatch in 5-10 days; maturity is reached in third or fourth year. Feeds on bottom-living invertebrates especially worms, molluscs and insect larvae.

WHITE BLEAK
Alburnus albidus
15 cm. Very similar to the bleak with an elongate body and flattened sides; conspicuously silvery. Head small, eye large and mouth oblique. Dorsal fin small, placed behind level of the pelvic fins, 7-8 branched rays. Anal fin long-based, with 13-17 branched rays. Scales large and fragile; 42-51 in lateral line. Sides silvery with a greyish-silver stripe from head to tail.
Distribution: Italy and the rivers of Yugoslavia, Albania and Greece.
Natural history: a schooling fish found in rivers, and in some lakes both large and small. Lives near the surface and is an active fish frequently seen as its shining sides glint in the light. Feeds on planktonic organisms, chiefly crustaceans and insect larvae, and takes insects at the surface.

A surface-living fish, the bleak uses its oblique mouth to take flies, midges and insects that fall into the water from bankside plants.

BLEAK
Alburnus alburnus

15 cm. A long slender fish with flattened sides and brilliantly silvery scales. Head small, eye large, mouth strongly oblique. Dorsal fin small, closer to tail than head; 8-9 branched rays. Anal fin long-based; 16-20 branched rays. Scales large and very easily dislodged; 48-55 in lateral line.

Distribution: widespread across western and central Europe from England to the Caspian basin; absent in northern Finland and Sweden, and the Iberian, Italian and Balkan peninsulas.

Natural history: forms large schools in slow-flowing rivers in lowland areas, keeping near and sometimes very close to the surface. Feeds on planktonic crustaceans, insect larvae and flying insects taken at the surface. Spawns May-June in shallow water over clean stones, occasionally on nearby vegetation. 5,000-6,500 eggs are shed by each female which hatch in 5-10 days. Bleak become sexually mature in 2-3 years.

SCHNEIDER
Alburnoides bipunctatus

15 cm. Similar to the bleak but deeper-bodied, head small and mouth terminal with jaws equal. Dorsal fin short-based but high, 9-11 branched rays, originating behind pelvic fins. Anal fin long-based, with 14-17 branched rays. Scales moderate in size, easily detached; 44-52 in lateral line. Coloration distinctive; olive green on back, sides silvery with yellowish band; lateral line shows up as double row of dark points.

Distribution: France, westward through the Danube system and into the rivers of the Black Sea basin.

Natural history: lives in small schools in medium-sized streams and, less often, in larger rivers. Always found in running water, which must be well-oxygenated, and prefers a hard, stony or rocky river bed. Spawns May-June on gravelly shallows, the eggs falling between the stones. Feeds on insect larvae (mainly bottom-living types) and adult insects at the surface, often ones which have fallen into the water.

DANUBIAN BLEAK
Chalcalburnus chalcoides
35 cm. Slender, streamlined body, similar to the bleak, with a small head, oblique mouth and prominent lower jaw. Sides compressed and flattened; a strongly compressed keel behind the pelvic fins. Dorsal fin short-based, medium-sized, placed above the space between pelvic and anal fins; 8-10 branched rays. Anal fin long-based; 15-20 branched rays. Scales small and well attached; 61-68 lateral line.

Distribution: Danube system and the rivers of the northern Black Sea and Caspian basins.

Natural history: very little is known of the biology of this species. Several populations live in large lakes in the Alps, but it is mainly a river fish. Lake populations live in shallow water over stony bottoms, retiring to deeper water in winter. In rivers they live in slow-flowing water in lowland reaches. Feeds on planktonic animals, principally crustaceans and insect larvae, but also eats a large number of insects at the surface. Breeds May-July.

ASP
Aspius aspius
60 cm. A slender-bodied fish with compressed sides and a sharp keel on the belly behind the vent. Head relatively large, mouth big and oblique, lower jaw prominent with a thickened tip which fits into a notch in the upper jaw. Scales small and firmly attached; 65-74 in lateral line. Anal fin high in front, concave in outline, with 12-14 branched rays.

Distribution: central and eastern Europe from West Germany eastwards; north to Sweden; throughout the Danube, and Black and Caspian Sea rivers.

Natural history: lives in lowland rivers and large lakes. Young fish form schools and feed on planktonic crustaceans and insect larvae. On reaching a length of 30 cm, the asp forms into loose aggregations and feeds on fishes. Spawns April-May in clean running water, the eggs falling between stones and hatching in 10-15 days. Larvae drift downstream into slow-flowing sheltered areas. Growth is quite fast: at the end of its first year it is 10-20 cm long; sexual maturity is attained in 4-5 years. This large, fish-eating member of the carp family has greatly diminished in numbers and is endangered in much of its range.

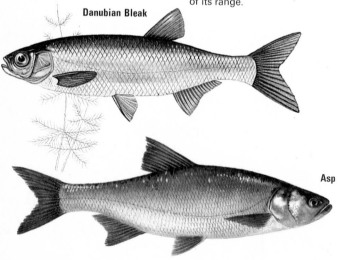

Danubian Bleak

Asp

BARBEL
Barbus barbus
91 cm. Long-bodied, rounded in cross-section but flat on the belly. Head large, large ventral mouth with thick fleshy lips and two pairs of long, fleshy barbels near the snout tip and at the mouth angle. Scales small, deeply embedded; 55-65 in lateral line. Dorsal fin short-based, high in front with a strong, serrated spine; anal fin short-based.

Distribution: central and eastern England, France, eastwards to the USSR. Absent in Scandinavia, the Iberian and Italian peninsulas.

Natural history: typically an inhabitant of rivers with a moderate gradient interspersed with quieter pools, and a clean bottom with sand and gravel. Such conditions also exist in lowland rivers below weirs and dams. A bottom-living fish, the barbel forages for food in the twilight and at night, feeding on bottom-living insect larvae, crustaceans, worms and molluscs. Forages in small groups but does not form schools. Spawns in late spring in medium depths, over gravel mixed with sand and pebbles. The yellowish eggs stick to the stones and hatch in 10-15 days; newly hatched fish stay in the gravel, but the young scatter in shallow running water close to the river's edge.

MEDITERRANEAN BARBEL
Barbus meridionalis
25 cm. Similar to the barbel in shape but with the head and back more arched. Four barbels round the mouth, the front pair long (bent back they reach past the nostril). Dorsal fin short-based, moderately high, with a strong, smooth-edged spine; anal fin short-based, long and pointed. Scales moderate in size, firmly attached; 48-55 in lateral line. Boldly marked with dark blotches on the back.

Distribution: southern France, northern Italy; said to occur in northern Spain. A separate subspecies in the Danube basin.

Natural history: a bottom-living fish typically found in clear running water over stones or gravel in the upper and middle reaches of rivers. Spawns May-July in running water over stones in shallows. Its food consists of bottom-living insect larvae, crustaceans, worms, and occasionally molluscs. Little is known of its biology and of the relations between the various populations.

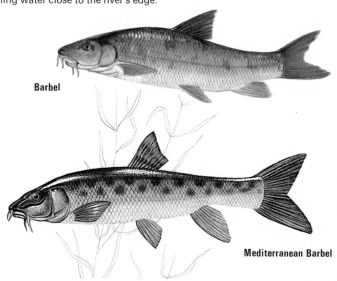

Barbel

Mediterranean Barbel

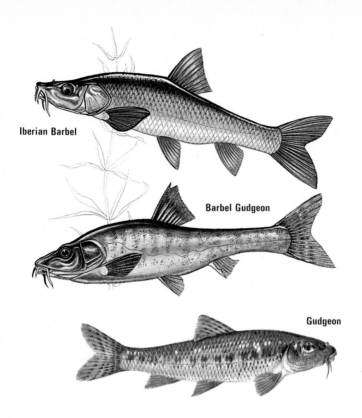

Iberian Barbel

Barbel Gudgeon

Gudgeon

GUDGEON
Gobio gobio
20 cm. Elongate but with a rounded body in cross-section, the tail flattened from side to side. Back slightly arched and belly flattened. Head broad, bluntly pointed, mouth ventral with one pair of barbels, one each side at the corner of the mouth. Dorsal fin short-based, moderately high; 9-10 branched rays. Anal fin short-based, low; 7–9 branched rays. Scales large, firmly attached; 38-44 in lateral line.

Distribution: throughout Europe, except for northern Finland and Sweden, Italy and the Adriatic coast rivers. Introduced to Spain, Ireland and Scotland.

Natural history: typically a river fish living in moderately fast-flowing streams to slow-flowing lowland rivers, but also occurs in large lakes, reservoirs and gravel pits and in low salinity areas of the Baltic. Sensitive to pollution and requires a high level of dissolved oxygen in the water, which influences its occurrence in certain polluted rivers as well as locally within the river. It is a bottom-living fish found usually in small, loose schools in shallow water on sandy and gravelly bottoms, less often on mud. Spawns on gravel or sand in running water, sometimes in shallows, the eggs adhering to stones and nearby plants. They hatch in 10-30 days depending on the temperature. Young fish are attracted to light and thus avoid sheltered crevices where mud accumulates. They form large schools in shallow water, which gradually disperse as they grow. Sexual maturity is reached in 2-3 years; few gudgeon live longer than 3 years although exceptional 6-7 year old fish have been recorded. Feeds on bottom-living insect larvae, crustaceans and worms; large fish even eat small molluscs. Numerous subspecies have been described from parts of Europe, but many are of doubtful validity.

IBERIAN BARBEL
Barbus comiza
50 cm. Similar to the barbel but with a flattened profile from the snout back to the dorsal fin. The head and snout are especially elongate. Four small barbels round the mouth. Scales moderate in size, firmly attached; 50-53 in lateral line.
Distribution: central and southern Portugal and Spain.
Natural history: virtually unknown but assumed to be similar to the Mediterranean barbel. The Iberian peninsula contains 5 or 6 species or subspecies of barbel, some of which are poorly known. Some are related to barbels found in southern Europe, while others seem closer to North African species, but much study is required before their identification is firmly established.

BARBEL GUDGEON
Aulopyge hugeli
13 cm. A slender-bodied fish, rounded in cross-section, with a long slender tail. Head rather large, eye small and placed near the dorsal outline; mouth terminal with four barbels; the first pair being small. The body is completely scaleless. The lateral line is distinct, running fairly centrally to the midline but curving up and down irregularly. Dorsal fin far down the back, with a stout serrated spine and 9 rays. Anal fin with a stout spine and 6 rays.
Distribution: occurs only in rivers in Bosnia and Dalmatia (Yugoslavia).
Natural history: a bottom-living fish found in rivers in Yugoslavia, but very little known. Said to eat invertebrates, especially worms and insects, but this could be claimed of any bottom-living freshwater fish. Probably an endangered species because of its restricted range.

The gudgeon lives on the bottom of rivers and lakes, both on stony and muddy beds; it has short barbels at the corners of its mouth.

WHITEFIN GUDGEON
Gobio albipinnatus
13 cm. Very similar in shape to the gudgeon, with a rather stout body rounded in cross-section, the tail fairly slender. Head rounded with a blunt snout and one pair of long barbels which reach behind the rear edge of the eye. Dorsal fin short-based and moderately high; 8-9 branched rays. Anal fin similar in shape; 7-8 branched rays. Scales large, firmly attached; 40-45 in lateral line. Throat and anterior belly scaleless. 8-10 dark blotches on the back and upper sides; the lateral line bordered above and below with fine dark points. Dorsal and tail fin without strong dark colouring.

Distribution: Danube basin from Germany and Austria downstream to the mouth. Also in the basins of the Don and Volga.

Natural history: relatively little known. Assumed to be similar to that of the gudgeon but known to live in the main stream of rivers, and thus occurs on soft bottoms in slowly-flowing areas. Also found in oxbow lakes and backwaters away from the flowing water. Is said to feed on crustaceans, insect larvae and worms.

KESSLER'S GUDGEON
Gobio kessleri
13 cm. Similar to the gudgeon but with a very slender body. In cross-section the body is rounded, although the belly is flat. Tail long and slender, especially just before the fin where it is rounded in cross-section. Head pointed, mouth moderate in size and ventral, with a very long barbel at the corner which reaches beyond the eye when laid flat. Dorsal fin moderate in size; 8 branched rays. Anal fin small, rounded; 7-8 branched rays. Scales large, firmly attached; 40-42 in lateral line, but absent on throat and anterior belly. Coloration brighter than the gudgeon tending to silvery; two rows of faint dark markings run parallel with the fork of the tail, the front row paler than the rear.

Distribution: in the Danube basin in both Austria and Germany eastwards to the delta: Also in the Dniester basin. Several subspecies of doubtful validity have been described.

Natural history: the natural history of this species is virtually unknown. Believed to be similar to that of the gudgeon, but it lives in more swiftly-flowing rivers and gravel bottoms. A bottom-living fish which probably eats more crustaceans than insect larvae.

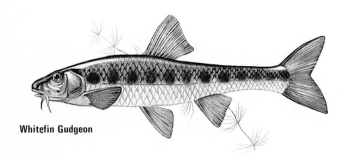

Whitefin Gudgeon

84

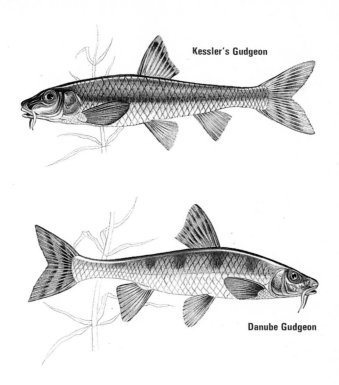

Kessler's Gudgeon

Danube Gudgeon

DANUBE GUDGEON
Gobio uranoscopus
15 cm. Similar to the gudgeon but very long and slender; rounded in cross-section although slightly flattened on the belly. Body in front of tail particularly narrow. Head pointed, mouth ventral with thick lips and a long barbel at the corner which, if depressed, reaches well beyond the level of the rear of the eye. Dorsal fin short-based and high; with 8-9 branched rays. Anal fin short-based and high; with 7–9 branched rays. Scales large, firmly attached. 40-43 in lateral line; throat and anterior belly covered with small scales. Colouring bold with 4-5 dark saddles across

the back which run down the sides; two clearly visible dark stripes on the tail fin running parallel to the edge.
Distribution: Danube basin, probably from Austria eastwards. Certainly in the tributaries in Czechoslovakia, Hungary, Romania and Yugoslavia.
Natural history: a bottom-living fish in the upper reaches of rivers where the current is fast and oxygen levels high. Highly sensitive to poor water quality. Its biology is not well known, but it is assumed to have a similar life-style to the other gudgeons, feeding on crustaceans and insect larvae. Said to breed May-June among stones in running water.

GRASS CARP
Ctenopharyngodon idella
1·25 m. Rather slender-bodied but with a large, broad, heavy head. Mouth terminal and large, lips well developed; eye placed low down on side of head. Dorsal and anal fins short-based, rounded; dorsal fin origin in front of pelvic base. Scales large, 43-45 in lateral line. Back greeny-brown, sides touched with gold, belly white; fins dusky.

Distribution: native to the River Amur and its flood-plain in China; now introduced to parts of eastern Europe and elsewhere.

Natural history: widely redistributed because of its feeding habits: as an adult it feeds exclusively on plants and so is used to keep navigable waterways free of excessive plant growth. In the USSR and much of eastern Europe it is also used for food. Spawns in the Amur in the main river channel in summer; the eggs, which are pelagic, are carried downstream, but on hatching find shelter in backwaters. In Europe most grass carp are raised in hatcheries.

SILVER CARP
Hypophthalmichthys molitrix
1 m. A deep-bodied fish with a large, broad head and a compressed belly. Sharp keel along underside. Mouth oblique, opening at the top of the head; eyes set slightly below level of mouth. Dorsal fin, high but short-based, originates behind base of pelvic fins. Anal fin long-based with a concave edge. Scales are small.

Distribution: native to China and the Amur basin; now widely distributed in Asia, the USSR and eastern Europe.

Natural history: feeds entirely on minute planktonic plants in the water; its gill rakers are attached to one another to form a fine-meshed sieve to strain the food out of the water. Migratory, the silver carp lives in the main channel of the Amur river while water flow is low and food abundant, but when the level rises it moves into flood-plain lakes. Spawning occurs in summer; the floating eggs are carried downstream until they hatch, when the larvae take shelter in inlets.

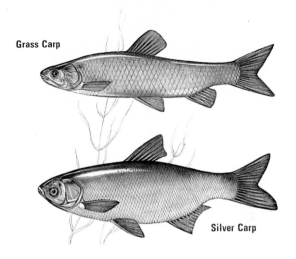

Grass Carp

Silver Carp

ZIEGE
Pelecus cultratus
50 cm. The body is moderately deep but the sides are strongly compressed so that it has a sharp keel running along the belly, which is curved, while the back is straight. Head small, mouth strongly oblique, opening on the top of the head. Dorsal fin small, placed far back; anal fin long-based, with 24-28 branched rays; pectoral fin long and pointed. Scales small, 95-115 in lateral line which is wavy.

Left: native to the rivers bordering China and the USSR, the grass carp was introduced to Europe for its weed-eating potential.

Distribution: two populations exist, one in the rivers of the eastern Baltic, occasionally extending into Sweden; the other in the Black Sea and Caspian Sea basins, notably in the River Danube.
Natural history: a gregarious fish which lives in large schools in brackish areas, lagoons, estuaries, and the lower reaches of rivers. Spawns in fresh water May-July, having migrated upstream from the river mouth. The eggs float, hatching in 2-3 days. Adults feed on small fishes, particularly young herring, gobies and small cyprinid fishes; young eat surface-living insects and planktonic crustaceans.

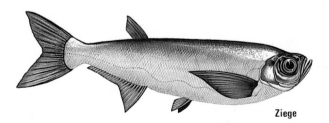

Ziege

TENCH

Tinca tinca

70 cm. A heavy-bodied, thickset fish with a small but broad head. The body, is deep and flattened, and compressed towards the tail. Mouth small and terminal, lips thick, with a single, rather small barbel at each corner of the mouth. Body covered with small scales, deeply embedded in the skin and covered with thick mucus; 87-115 in lateral line. Fins rounded; dorsal and anal fins short-based – dorsal fin with 10-11 branched rays; anal fin with 8-10 branched rays. Males have the second ray (the first full-length ray) of the pelvic fin thickened and fleshy; the pelvic rays are longer in males than in females. Coloration a deep greeny-brown above and on the sides, often with a golden tinge on the belly; fins dark brown.

Distribution: widespread across Europe from Ireland to central USSR. Absent in northern Europe, from southern Sweden northwards and along the Adriatic coastline of the Balkans. Widely introduced, it is not native to Ireland or the Iberian peninsula.

Natural history: the tench is a secretive fish which lives close to the bottom, sometimes actually in the bottom when it buries itself during cold winters. It lives in still waters mostly lakes, ponds, oxbows, and occasionally in the slow-flowing reaches of lowland rivers. Man-made still-water habitats such as reservoirs, gravel pits and canals have increased its distribution and the latter have allowed it to disperse widely. It can tolerate slightly salt conditions and is occasionally found in the lower reaches of estuaries. It is very tolerant of low levels of dissolved oxygen and can survive in summer where dense weed growth and organic matter reduce the level of oxygen to almost zero. Also tolerates the cold, but spawning may be delayed by very cold winters. Spawns in late spring and early summer, the eggs being laid on plant leaves and stems underwater. 300,000-900,000 eggs are laid by each female, depending on her size. The eggs measure 0·8-1·0 mm in diameter and are laid in batches at about two week intervals. They hatch in 6-8 days. The larvae, which are 4-5 mm long, have an adhesive organ on the head by means of which they hang attached to the plants while the yolk of the egg is absorbed. About 10 days after hatching they begin to feed on rotifers, crustacean larvae, and other small animals. As they grow they eat larger invertebrates, particularly bottom-living insect larvae, ostracods, worms and molluscs. All through their lives they eat considerable quantities of plant matter. In rich waters where food is abundant the tench can grow moderately fast – up to 30 cm in 3 years. However, as many of the waters in which the tench can live are not satisfactory habitats, this growth rate is often not attained. A valuable food fish in eastern Europe, partly because its low requirements of oxygen mean that it can be transported out of water while still alive. This also permits its artificial distribution.

Tench

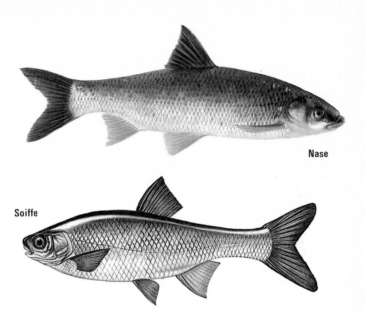

Nase

Soiffe

NASE
Chondrostoma nasus
50 cm. A slender-bodied fish, rather compressed at the sides. Head small, snout protuberant and rounded. Mouth inferior, the upper lip thick and fleshy, the lower lip a sharp-edged horny blade. The mouth opening is virtually straight. Dorsal and anal fins moderately high but short-based; dorsal with 10-13 branched rays; anal with 10-12 branched rays. Scales moderate in size; 57-62 in lateral line. When spawning the gill covers and the bases of pectoral and pelvic fins become red.
Distribution: central Europe from France eastwards to the Caspian Sea.
Natural history: a schooling fish, living in fast flowing rivers, often far up towards their headwaters, and requiring well-oxygenated water. Locally common below weirs downstream. Feeds on green algae and diatoms growing on rocks – its blade-like lower jaw being well suited for scraping up such food. Spawns in March in small tributaries over gravel in shallow water, when schools gather with much splashing. Maturity is reached in 3-4

years and the nase's maximum life span is about 10 years.

SOIFFE
Chondrostoma toxostoma
25 cm. Slender-bodied with a small head and rounded protuberant snout. The mouth is small, ventral and horseshoe-shaped with a horny, sharp-edged lower lip. Dorsal and anal fins short-based, 9 branched rays in former, 8-9 in latter. Scales moderate in size; 54-59 in lateral line. A diffuse dark line runs from head to tail.
Distribution: found only in southern France, and in some Spanish and Portuguese rivers.
Natural history: lives in small rivers, sometimes in lakes, but only where oxygen levels are high and the bottom clean. Also found in the small tributaries in which the nase spawns. Spawning takes place in early spring in gravelly shallows after migration upstream. Feeds on green algae and diatom films growing over rocks. The Iberian populations may be subspecifically distinct from the French ones.

LASKA NASE
Chondrostoma genei
30 cm. Slender-bodied with a small head and blunt rounded snout. Mouth small and ventral, the lower lip with a horny blade on its edge. Dorsal and anal fins short-based, rather low; dorsal with 8 branched rays, anal with 8-9. Scales are moderately small, 52-58 in lateral line. A dark band runs from the pectoral fin base to the tail fin just above the lateral line.
Distribution: lives in rivers in northern and central Italy, principally the Po catchment. Reported at one time in the headwaters of the upper Rhine and the Danube, but this is now thought to be erroneous.
Natural history: lives mostly in the middle reaches of large rivers, often in weir pools where oxygen levels are locally raised. Migrates into tributaries to spawn March-May in shallow water over gravel beds. Feeds mainly on green algae encrusting rocks and wooden pilings, but also eats some invertebrates. Is possibly no more than a local race – maybe a subspecies – of the soiffe.

ITALIAN NASE
Chondrostoma soetta
40 cm. A stout nase, its maximum body depth being more than a quarter of its body length (in most nases it is much less). Head small, snout bluntly rounded, mouth almost terminal. Lips strongly arched, the lower lip with a hard horny covering. Dorsal fin short-based, with 8-9 branched rays; anal fin longer-based with 11-13 branched rays. 55-63 scales in lateral line. Back blue-green, belly silvery with a yellowish tinge; no broad dark stripe on sides; pelvic and anal fins reddish.
Distribution: found only in northern Italy, mainly in the basin of the river Po, but also in lakes.
Natural history: generally confined to the middle reaches of the larger rivers. Lives in schools close to the bottom and feeds on encrusting green algae and invertebrates. In its biology and general appearance this fish is very similar to the nase; it may be only a subspecies of that form.

IBERIAN NASE
Chondrostoma polylepis
25 cm. Slender-bodied with a small head and bluntly-pointed conical snout. Mouth ventral, lips thickened although the lower lip has a horny, sharp-edged blade. Dorsal and anal fins short-based and rather low; the dorsal has 8 branched rays; the anal 9-10. Scales on the body small; 69-74 on lateral line.
Distribution: lives only in the rivers of Portugal and central Spain. Occasionally found in lakes.
Natural history: feeds on encrusting algae, diatoms and invertebrates which live on rocks and stones in the river bed. Spawns in spring on gravel in shallow water, and occasionally on timber pilings in the river bed. A subspecies, possibly a closely related species, *C. polylepis willkommi* (found in southern Spanish rivers) is distinguished by having rather fewer but larger scales; 60-68 in lateral line.

PARDILLA NASE
Chondrostoma lemmingii
15 cm. Slender-bodied with a small head and slightly ventral mouth. The mouth is arched and the lower lip has a hard, horny edge to it. Dorsal and anal fins short-based and rounded; dorsal fin with 7 branched rays, anal fin with 7-8 branched rays. Scales moderate in size; 58-69 in lateral line. Back dark olive-green, with a dusky stripe running from head to tail; sides brilliantly silver; fins yellowish except for the dusky bases of the pectoral and dorsal.
Distribution: found only in the rivers of Portugal and south-eastern Spain.
Natural history: the pardilla nase lives in schools in slow-flowing rivers and lowland lakes. Is said to spawn April-May in large schools over weed in shallows. This species was for a long time placed in either *Leuciscus* or *Rutilus* and has only recently been found to be a nase. Much of its reported biology is not in keeping with that of other *Chondrostoma* species, and requires confirmation.

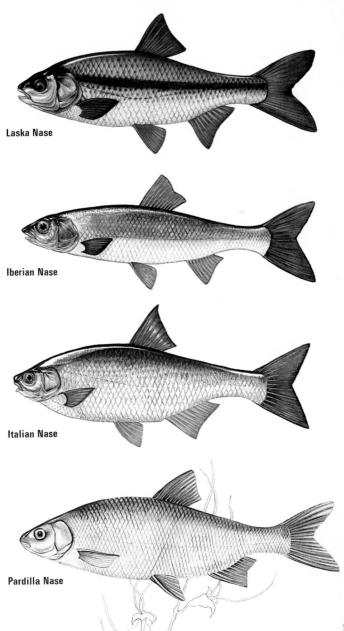

Laska Nase

Iberian Nase

Italian Nase

Pardilla Nase

91

LOACH FAMILY
Cobitidae

Loaches are mostly small to medium-sized fishes, the largest growing to about 30 cm. They are usually slender-bodied, some almost eel-like in shape, although most are compressed from side to side. They are restricted to Europe, Asia and parts of northern Africa, and are strictly confined to fresh water. Most loaches are bottom-living and have three or more pairs of barbels which, though short in some species, are mostly rather long, and are used for detecting food. Most also have small eyes set near the upper profile of the head. Loaches are related to the carp family and, like them, have no spines in their fins, scaleless heads (many loaches are completely scaleless), and no teeth in their jaws. They have numerous pharyngeal teeth in a single row on each pharyngeal bone. The front part of the swimbladder is always enclosed in a bony capsule which connects to the inner ear on each side. It seems likely that loaches are very sensitive to sounds underwater, but little is known about this aspect of their biology. Some of them can detect changes in atmospheric pressure – presumably also by means of the specialized swimbladder.

The loaches are a successful group of fishes, having colonized many freshwater habitats, from fast-flowing hill streams to still and stagnant ponds. Some of those living in ponds have the ability to gulp air at the surface and so absorb oxygen through the gut – a useful accomplishment for fishes living in oxygen-poor environments.

Spined Loach

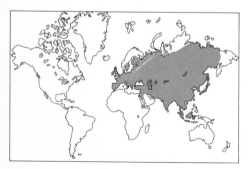

About 150 species of loach are recognized, with the greatest number in tropical Asia. All are small freshwater fishes; some are worm-like and many bury themselves in the river bed.

SPINED LOACH
Cobitis taenia

12 cm. Body elongate and strongly compressed from side to side; head small and also compressed, with the eye placed high on the top of the head. Mouth small, ventral, with six short barbels on the lips. Dorsal fin small, placed about midway along the body; small anal fin near the tail. A small doubled-pointed spine hidden in a groove under each eye can be detected by running a finger from tail to nose.

Distribution: found across the whole of Europe and central Asia, except for northern regions. Lives in eastern England only.

Natural history: lives buried in soft

The stone loach usually hides under rocks or in dense weed in daylight and forages for food in the twilight.

mud in slow-flowing rivers and drains, and occasionally lakes in river flood-plains. Is highly sensitive to the particle size of the mud, which has to be fine. Also burrows in green filamentous algae on the river bed. Feeds by sucking in mud and swirling it around the gill chamber, so that the edible parts – bacteria, nematode worms and plant fragments – stick to the mucus on the throat and are swallowed, while the mud is puffed out through the gill opening. Spawns April-June, the eggs being laid on filamentous algae.

STONE LOACH
Noemacheilus barbatulus
15 cm. Slender-bodied, rounded in cross-section in front, but flattened from side to side at the tail. Head moderate-sized with a fairly large eye; the ventral mouth has 6 long barbels around the lips. No spine beneath the eye. Dorsal and anal fins short-based, rounded and rather small.

Distribution: widely distributed from Ireland (where it was introduced) across Europe and Asia to China. Absent in the Italian and Iberian peninsulas.

Natural history: lives in rivers and less often lakes. In rivers it is most abundant in small streams with stony beds, but also occurs on muddy bottoms among water plants. During the day it hides among water plants or under stones, emerging at night to feed on small crustaceans, insect larvae, and botttom-living invertebrates. Breeds April-June, shedding its dull white eggs among stones and water plants in several separate spawnings. The eggs hatch in 14-16 days at temperatures of 12-16°C. The young fish reach maturity at 2-3 years and may live for as long as 7 years. Because it is relatively sensitive to pollution and low oxygen levels, the stone loach's presence in a river can be taken as an indication of good water quality.

POND LOACH
Misgurnus fossilis
35 cm. Long, slender body, rounded in cross-section. Head small, mouth small and terminal with 5 pairs of barbels, those on the lower lip being smallest. Dorsal fin small and rounded, nearer to the tail fin than the head; anal fin very small and rounded; tail fin rounded, large. Dull brown with dark horizontal lines; very slimy.

Distribution: eastern and central Europe from the river Rhine to the Caspian Sea basin.

Natural history: lives in still waters, shallow ponds, small lakes with muddy bottoms, and swamps. In such oxygen-poor waters it survives by gulping at the surface and swallowing the air, about half the oxygen in which is then absorbed by the strongly folded lining of the gut. In very dry weather this loach buries into the mud and aestivates. Its breathing of atmospheric air means that it is sensitive to changes of barometric pressure. Before thunderstorms it becomes very active, gulping at the surface – the reason it is known as the weather fish. Spawns April-June, each female depositing some 70,000 eggs on plants in shallow water. For a few days after hatching the young fish have long thread-like external gills – another adaptation to life in poorly-oxygenated water.

GOLDEN LOACH
Cobitis aurata
12 cm. Body elongate and compressed but relatively deep (the body depth is greater than the length of the head). Head small, with a small terminal mouth and six moderately long barbels branched on their rear edge. Tail in front of tail fin with a fleshy ridge above and below. Dorsal and anal fins short-based, relatively small, with 7 and 5 branched rays respectively. Double-pointed spine on cheek beneath eye.

Distribution: occurs only in the Danube basin and in the rivers of the Black and Caspian Seas.

Natural history: inhabits the upper reaches of rivers and streams among weed beds and buries in coarse sandy bottoms. Feeds on bottom-living insect larvae, small crustaceans and worms. Spawns May-July.

ITALIAN LOACH
Cobitis larvata
8 cm. Elongate and compressed but deep-bodied, the greatest depth being just behind the pectoral fin base, and deeper than the head is long. Mouth small with six barbels, the last longest. A small, double-pointed spine under the eye. Ridges above and below the tail just in front of the fin. Dusky blotches each side of the tail fin base.

Distribution: northern Italy only, around Venice and the river Po basin.

Natural history: lives buried in mud in the lower reaches of rivers and lagoons. Breeds May-July, the eggs being laid among plants and algae on the river bed. Its food consists of minute organic items found in the surface of the mud.

Stone Loach

Pond Loach

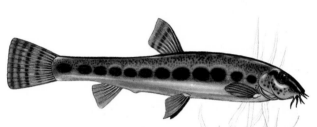

Golden Loach

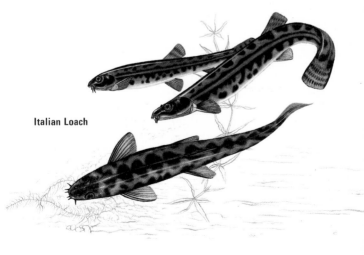

Italian Loach

CATFISH FAMILY
Siluridae

Catfishes belong to the order Siluriformes, which comprises an estimated 2,000 species of mainly freshwater fishes. The order is best represented in South America where about half the species are found, but there are also a number of species in the rivers and lakes of Africa, Asia and North America. Europe is poorly inhabited: only two catfishes are native, although several have been introduced from North America.

Most catfishes are bottom-living fishes; this is suggested by the shape of their body, which is flat on the underside to ensure close contact with the bottom. However, a number of tropical species are surface-living, or at any rate live in mid-water and in these the body is differently shaped. Catfishes are usually scaleless, and their skin is thick and slimy, although paradoxically, the exceptions have bodies covered in heavy, bony plates. Many catfishes are crepuscular or nocturnal in their life-style and have small eyes, which are presumably not of much use to fish active in the dark and living near the bottom. However, all species have long, highly sensitive barbels which are of great value in this habitat. The two native European catfishes belong to the family Siluridae, which is also represented in Asia. They have long barbels on the upper jaw, a minute dorsal fin set close behind the head, no adipose fin and a long-based, many-rayed anal fin.

Wels

A family with numerous species, most abundant in tropical Asia. The European species are on the extreme edge of its range, but the wels has been redistributed by man into western Europe.

WELS
Silurus glanis
3 m. Long, slender body with a very broad head and barrel-shaped belly. Eyes minute; mouth terminal with the lower jaw protuberant, an extremely long barbel rising on the upper jaw and two shorter barbels on each side of the lower jaw. Dorsal fin extremely small, short-based. In contrast to anal fin, it runs from the vent almost to the tail fin.
Distribution: the wels is confined to Europe from the river Rhine eastwards to the Black and Caspian Seas. Absent from the Iberian, Italian and Balkan peninsulas, and from the British Isles, although it has been introduced to England.
Natural history: lives in slow-flowing rivers and large still waters, particularly those in lowland areas. Tolerates slightly salt water and can be found in areas of low salinity in parts of the Baltic and Black Seas. Largely nocturnal, mostly feeding soon after sunset and just before dawn, but is active during the day in heavily silted rivers. Lives close to the bottom, in

Europe's largest freshwater fish, the wels is not often seen, even where it is common, as it hides during daylight in crevices. The long barbels help it find its food when hunting at night.

hollows under overhanging banks, among tree roots or beneath fallen trees on the river or lake bed. It feeds mainly on fishes, especially eels, burbot, tench and roach, but it also takes ducklings and water voles. Eats aquatic insects and crustaceans when young. Breeds May-July, when the eggs are laid in a shallow depression excavated by the male fish. Growth is rapid; the young become mature at 4-5 years and may live for up to 20 years.

97

ARISTOTLE'S CATFISH
Silurus aristotelis

1·5 m. Long-bodied, compressed from side to side from the vent to the tail fin, but the body is cylindrical and the head flattened. Small dorsal fin on the back above and just behind the pectoral fins; long anal fin. A long barbel on each upper jaw bone; a pair of shorter barbels under the chin.

Distribution: lives only in the basin of the River Akelhoos in Greece.

Natural history: an inhabitant of slow-flowing rivers and lakes, Aristotle's catfish feeds on fishes when adult and bottom-living invertebrates when young. Spawns July-August in a shallow hollow made by the male, who guards the eggs until they hatch.

AMERICAN CATFISH FAMILY
Ameiuridae

Native to North America, this family of catfishes has been widely distributed in other continents, including Europe. Most of the forty species or so known in North America look like typical catfishes, with broad heads, cylindrical bodies and flattened tails, and numerous long barbels round the mouth. In this family, there are eight barbels on the head, two on the nostrils, two

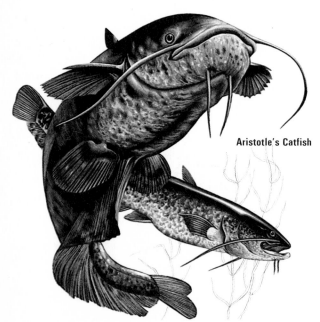

Aristotle's Catfish

on the upper jaw and four on the chin. The dorsal fin is short-based and rounded, with a stout spine in the front of the fin, and there is a similar spine on the leading edge of each pectoral fin.

98

BLACK BULLHEAD
Ictalurus melas
30 cm. Stout-bodied with a broad flattened head; the tail flattened from side to side. Mouth large and terminal; four pairs of barbels on the head. Dorsal fin small, short-based; a long low adipose fin on the back: anal fin long, with 17-21 rays. The rear edge of the pectoral fin spines only slightly barbed at the base.
Distribution: eastern North America; introduced to Europe and now common in western and central Europe.
Natural history: lives on soft muddy bottoms in lowland streams and lakes. Spawns in summer in a nest excavated in the bottom by the female; both male and female guard the eggs, which hatch in about 5 days.

BROWN BULLHEAD
Ictalurus nebulosus
36 cm. Very similar to the Black Bullhead. The main distinguishing features are that the anal fin has 21-24 rays, and the rear edge of the pectoral fin spines is deeply serrated almost to the tip.
Distribution: eastern North America; introduced to, and locally common in, parts of western Europe.
Natural history: very similar to that of the Black Bullhead. In Europe there is evidence that the two species have bred together to produce hybrids. Both the species and their hybrids are common in northern Italy, a centre for the breeding of goldfish, and from there are widely exported both as pond fish and as experimental animals.

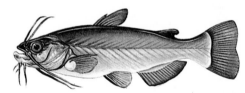

Black Bullhead

Brown Bullhead

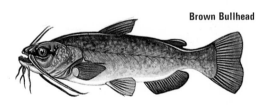

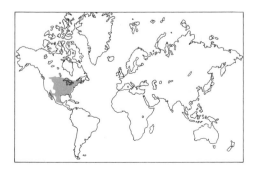

There are 37 species in this family, all native to North America. Several have been introduced to other parts of the world, including Europe. All are freshwater fishes.

CODFISH FAMILY
Gadidae

Of the fifty-five or so species in the codfish family, all but one, the burbot, live in the sea. Codfishes are particularly numerous in the cooler waters of the northern hemisphere, only a few species occurring south of the Equator. Most live in the shallower waters of the continental shelf, some are found in deep water but several live on the shore. All are slender-bodied fishes with large heads and have a chin barbel. Some have other barbels around the head. Many codfishes have three dorsal and two anal fins, among them the cod and the haddock, but others have only a short first dorsal fin followed by a long-based second dorsal; the anal fin is also long-based. The pelvic fins are placed well forward, in front of the level of the pectoral fin base.

BURBOT
Lota lota
1 m. Long-bodied, with a broad head and large terminal mouth. A long chin barbel; shorter barbels on the anterior nostrils. Two dorsal fins, the first short-based and rounded, the second long-based, like the anal fin.
Distribution: from eastern England eastwards across Europe, southern Europe, and the rest of the British Isles.
Natural history: lives in lowland rivers and lakes, usually hiding among tree roots or under over-hanging banks, but becoming active at dawn and in the evening. Young burbot feed on crustaceans, particularly the water hog louse, crayfish, and insects. The adults eat larger crayfish and all kinds of fishes, especially injured or diseased fish. Breeds December-March, under the ice, over gravel beds, the female laying up to 3 million eggs. Almost buoyant, the eggs float just above the bottom and so do not get buried by mud.

Burbot

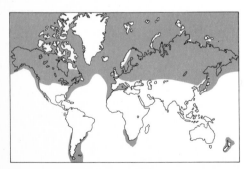

There are about 55 species in the family, all marine fishes except for the burbot. Most members of the family are shallow-water fishes, many of great commercial importance.

TOOTHCARP FAMILY
Cyprinodontidae

The toothcarps are a large family of mostly small fishes found in all tropical and warm temperate parts of the world, except for Australia. Though somewhat similar to the carp family, they are not closely related – one of the important differences being that they have teeth in their jaws. As a group, they are adaptable little fishes, able to live in freshwater pools and to tolerate extreme heat, as well as highly saline and alkaline pools.

SPANISH TOOTHCARP
Aphanius iberus
5 cm. A stout little fish with a single, short-based, rounded dorsal fin opposite the similar shaped anal fin. Head broad, mouth oblique, opening at the upper side of head. Males have about 15 light, distinct crossbars along back and sides and a tail fin with 4 vertical brown bars; females have 2-4 scattered rows of spots on body and uncoloured fins.
Distribution: occurs only in the coastal areas of south-east Spain and North Africa.
Natural history: lives in brackish lagoons and river mouths, ditches and swamps. Feeds on small crustaceans and insect larvae, especially mosquitos. Breeds in summer, the 200 or so eggs being laid among plants and hatching in 2 weeks.

SOUTH EUROPEAN TOOTHCARP
Aphanius fasciatus
6 cm. A chunky little fish with a broad head. Wide mouth set on the upper side of the head. Dorsal fin moderately long-based with 10-12 rays; anal fin shorter with 8-10 rays. Males with 10-15 dusky transverse bars on sides and a broad dark band on the edge of the tail. Females have narrower, less distinct bars and greyish fins.
Distribution: coastal lagoons and marshy areas of the Mediterranean from France eastwards.
Natural history: in brackish and saline pools in coastal areas. Feeds on small crustaceans and insect larvae. Breeds in spring and summer. The related Valencia toothcarp *(Valencia hispanica)* lives in similar habitats in southern Spain.

male

female

Spanish Toothcarp

South European Toothcarp

Most members of the family live in fresh and brackish water, with a few marine coastal species. The toothcarps are most numerous in tropical regions. There are at least 300 species; all lay eggs.

LIVEBEARER FAMILY
Poecilidae

The livebearers are a large family of small fishes native to America. They live in a variety of habitats from saline pools on the coast to weedy streams far inland. Their success is due to their reproductive habits of giving birth to live young – the females, which are larger than the males, carrying the eggs until they are ready to hatch, when they are expelled and the young fish swim free. Male livebearers have the first few rays of the anal fin modified into the gonopodium by means of which sperm is transferred to the female.

GUPPY
Porecilia reticulata
6 cm. Small with a broad head, the mouth opening at the upper edge of the head. Dorsal and anal fins short-based and rounded. Aquarium bred males are very colourful; wild fish less so.
Distribution: native to Trinidad and north-eastern South America, now occurs in many parts of the world including Europe.
Natural history: lives in still waters in isolated parts of southern Europe, and in the north where temperatures are artificially raised by power station effluents and the like. Gives birth to 5-20 young in frequent breeds.

MOSQUITO FISH
Gambusia affinis
6 cm. Small slender fishes with a narrow pointed head and terminal mouth opening. Both sexes are pale greeny-grey on the back and upper sides, with flecks of darker colouring; ventrally they are silvery white; a dusky bar runs vertically through the eye.
Distribution: native to south-eastern North America; introduced to southern Europe and now common around the Mediterranean basin.
Natural history: lives in still waters, pools, ditches and brackish lagoons. Breeds through summer, giving birth to 30-50 young in each brood.

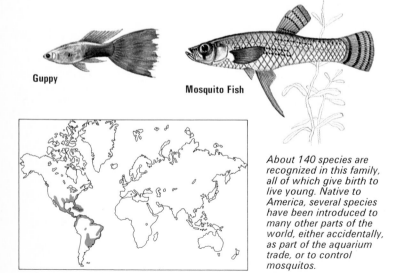

Guppy

Mosquito Fish

About 140 species are recognized in this family, all of which give birth to live young. Native to America, several species have been introduced to many other parts of the world, either accidentally, as part of the aquarium trade, or to control mosquitos.

SILVERSIDE FAMILY
Atherinidae

Most members of this fairly large family are small fishes. The majority are characterized by the bright silvery stripe along the sides and white belly which gives them their common name. They are slender-bodied fishes, usually with large eyes, and a protrusile, terminal mouth. Their bodies are covered with large fragile scales and they have two dorsal fins, the first consisting of slender spines, the second of one or two spines and several branched rays. The single anal fin is similar to the second dorsal. Once considered to be relatives of the grey mullets, silversides are now thought to be related to the toothcarps and livebearers. Mostly marine fishes of tropical and temperate seas, but some live entirely in fresh water.

BIG-SCALE SANDSMELT
Atherina boyeri

12 cm. A long slender fish with two well-separated dorsal fins, the first composed of thin, rather delicate spines, and fairly high; the second triangular in shape with a short spine and 10-12 branched rays. Anal fin similar in shape with 2 spines and 11-13 branched rays. Head small, mouth large and oblique with jaws that extend forwards. Body scales large, 44-48 in series from head to tail fin; very easily dislodged. Bright silvery sides; white ventrally.

Distribution: coastal waters from southern England and Holland southwards to the Mediterranean and the Black Sea.

Natural history: in northern Europe this sandsmelt is probably a summer migrant; in the Mediterranean it is abundant in shallow brackish lagoons and coastal marshes, as well as in estuaries and even in fresh water. Feeds on planktonic animals, chiefly crustaceans, and fish larvae. Breeds April-August, usually close to green filamentous algae to which the eggs stick by long threads. Some 600 eggs are produced annually by each female and shed in batches.

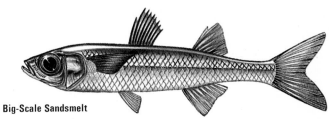

Big-Scale Sandsmelt

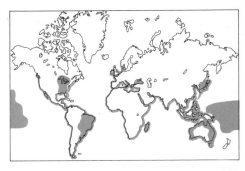

The family consists mainly of inshore marine fishes which swim in tightly packed schools. Some are abundant in estuaries and low salinity lagoons, and others live in fresh water. There are about 150 species, mostly tropical.

STICKLEBACK FAMILY
Gasterosteidae

The sticklebacks form a very distinctive family which is found both in the sea and in fresh water virtually across the whole northern hemisphere. Small fishes, with elongate to torpedo-shaped bodies, they are always scaleless, although some species have a number of flat bony plates on their sides, which vary in number according to local circumstances. They have two dorsal fins, the first comprising a series of isolated spines, varying in number from 2 or 3 to 15–18 according to species, and the second a normal fin of branched rays with a short spine in front. The anal fin is similar to the second dorsal fin. Pectoral fins are well-developed and play a considerable part in helping the fish swim, but the pelvic fins are reduced to a single sharp spine each side. Sticklebacks live mostly in still waters, such as ponds, lakes and ditches, but are also common in lowland rivers and streams. Some species are wholly marine and live in coastal waters, while others, like the Three-spined Stickleback, can live in fresh water, brackish water, and in the sea. Like several other sticklebacks, the Three-spined is a variable form, changing in appearance with its habitat and genetic composition.

Three-spined Stickleback

Ten-spined Stickleback

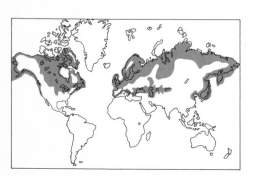

Eight species are recognized in this family, but this takes no account of the complex variations in several species groups. The sticklebacks live in the sea, especially in northern waters, and in brackish and fresh waters.

THREE-SPINED STICKLEBACK
Gasterosteus aculeatus
10 cm. Body moderately deep, although very slender at the tail. Head relatively large and pointed, with a small, protrusile mouth. Three sharp spines on the back, the third is the smallest and is close to the second dorsal fin. Pelvic fins a strong, sharp spine with a minute ray. Body scaleless, but often with a few broad scutes near the end, and sometimes a complete row each side. Males have conspicuous red throats in breeding season.
Distribution: coastal areas of northern North America and Europe; widely distributed in western and northern Europe.
Natural history: occurs in the sea in northern Europe, but mainly known as an inhabitant of ditches, ponds, lakes and rivers. Often very abundant. Breeds in spring and summer, the male building a nest and enticing a female into it to lay eggs, then guarding nest and young against competitors and predators. The nest is built on the bottom out of plant fibres. Feeds on small crustaceans, insect larvae, worms, small fish larvae and molluscs, and is itself eaten in numbers by kingfishers, herons, and fishes such as pike.

NINE-SPINED STICKLEBACK
Pungitius pungitius
7 cm. Body rather slender with a long, narrow section just before the tail fin; head small, mouth oblique and protrusile. First dorsal fin with 8-10 (usually 9) sharp spines; second dorsal and anal fins low and of similar shape. Pelvic fin reduced to a short spine. Breeding males have a black throat and pale blue pelvic fin spines.
Distribution: across much of northern North America and Europe, mainly confined to lowlands within 200 miles of the coast.
Natural history: widely distributed but rather local and tends to be found in ponds, ditches and small streams which have a dense covering of plants. Very resistant to low oxygen levels, and sometimes found in swamps. Builds a nest of plant fibres about 7-10 cm off the bottom; the male builds and guards the nest and entices the female to lay eggs in it. Feeds on small crustaceans and insect larvae. Maximum life span about 3 years.

In spring the male stickleback develops a bright red throat and belly used to display to the female and to keep other males at a distance.

BULLHEAD FAMILY
Cottidae

The bullhead family comprises a large number of marine fishes found in cool and temperate seas, as well as numerous freshwater fishes living in the northern hemisphere. Most are heavy-bodied, stout-headed fishes with numerous spines on the head.

BULLHEAD
Cottus gobio
10 cm. Broad, flattened head with a sharp curved spine on the front of the gill cover. Two dorsal fins, the first smaller than the second. Pectoral fin broad; pelvic fins pale.
Distribution: eastwards from Wales and England to eastern Europe.
Natural history: abundant in streams, small rivers and large stony-bottomed lakes. Usually in shallow water under large stones or in dense weed beds. Feeds at night, mainly on crustaceans and bottom-living insect larvae. Spawns March-May under stones, the eggs being guarded for 3-4 weeks until they hatch. May live for up to 5 years.

SIBERIAN BULLHEAD
Cottus poecilopus
10 cm. Similar to Bullhead, but lateral line pores have openings only as far as the level of the second dorsal fin. Pelvic fins are long, reaching to beyond the vent; the innermost ray is very short
Distribution: southern Scandinavia eastwards into the northern USSR.
Natural history: lives in stony-bottomed streams mostly in the upland reaches, and in large lakes. Feeds on crustaceans and insect larvae. Breeds February-April, spawning in nests under stones – the eggs being stuck to the roof of the nest.

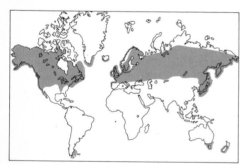

This family contains both marine and freshwater fishes, although some marine species enter rivers to feed, especially when young.

Siberian Bullhead

Bullhead

SEA BASS FAMILY
Percichthyidae

The sea basses are now considered to belong to the family Percichthyidae, which contains an assortment of marine and freshwater fishes. The European basses are found in estuaries and penetrate into fresh water when young. They are slender-bodied, strong-swimming fishes with large scales and two dorsal fins, the first of which has strong spines. The anal fin has three stout spines before the branched rays, and the pelvics have one spine and five soft rays. They have a series of strong, forward-pointing spines on the lower edge of the front part of the gill cover.

Bass

BASS
Dicentrarchus labrax
1 m. A slender-bodied, streamlined, silvery fish with two dorsal fins, the first comprised of 8-9 strong, slender spines, the second of a spine and 12-13 branched rays. Anal fin with 3 spines and 10-11 branched rays. Scales moderately small, present on most of the head and all the body; 66-74 in the lateral line. Strong forward pointing spines on the edge of the gill cover below the eye.
Distribution: in coastal waters from southern Norway southwards to North Africa then through the Mediterranean.
Natural history: a sea fish which is very common in river mouths and estuaries, and penetrates into fresh water. Migrates in schools in northern waters, entering shallow waters and estuaries mainly in summer. Feeds on a wide range of smaller fishes and crustaceans. Breeds in spring in British inshore waters; the eggs and early larvae float near the surface. In the Mediterranean, the Spotted Bass *(Dicentrarchus punctatus)*, distinguished by its heavily speckled back, is also common in brackish water.

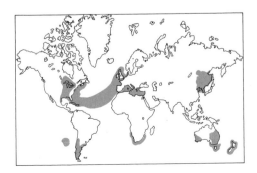

There are around 300 species in this family; most are marine fish from coastal waters, but some occur in deep water. Most freshwater species live in North America, several in northern Asia.

107

BLACK BASS FAMILY
Centrarchidae

Black basses or Sunfishes are Northern American freshwater fishes which have been widely distributed in Europe and other parts of the world. Several species, like the black basses, are considered to be good sporting fish and have been introduced as fish for anglers. Others, like the sunfishes, are brightly coloured and are kept in cold water aquaria or ponds, and have either escaped or been deliberately released into the wild. In some parts of Europe, where they have become locally abundant, they have adversely affected native fishes, for they are both predators on, and competitors with, other species. Most members of the family are fairly stout, fully-scaled fishes, with a dorsal fin composed of strong sharp spines – most with about 10 spines, but varying from 5 to 13 – and longer branched rays. The anal fin is also composed of spines, 3–7 depending on the species, and soft rays. Most sunfishes are nest builders: the male hollows out a shallow depression by flicking his tail and throwing sand or mud out to settle away from the nest or, in rivers, to be carried downstream. The eggs are laid in the nest after an extensive courtship and, being adhesive, they settle on the clean exposed stones of the nest. The eggs and early larvae are guarded by the male, but once the young have absorbed the yolk of the egg and are actively swimming, they leave the male's territory.

ROCK BASS
Ambloplites rupestris
30 cm. A deep-bodied sunfish, with a rather large head and a large mouth, terminal, but slightly angled. Dorsal fin continuous with 10-12 stout, sharp spines, almost the same length as the succeeding branched rays. Anal fin also continuous, the 6 spines of gradually increasing length joined to the first of the ten branched rays. Scales moderate in size, firmly attached; 37-51 in the lateral line.

Distribution: widespread in eastern central North America; found in southern England, and may well occur sporadically in continental Europe.

Natural history: in North America lives in shallow lakes and slow flowing lowland streams, preferring areas where the bottom is rocky. Feeds mainly on the larvae of aquatic insects,

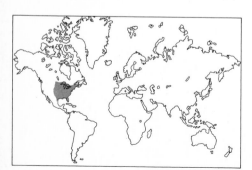

There are 30 species in this exclusively North American family. Several have been introduced to Europe and other parts of the world, and have established a strong presence.

crustaceans, and small fishes. Spawns May-July in a shallow nest up to 61 cm in diameter, excavated by the male in sand or gravel. 3,000-11,000 eggs are laid in the nest and guarded by the male. They hatch in 3-4 days. Sexually mature in 3-4 years, the rock bass may live for up to 10 years.

PUMPKINSEED
Lepomis gibbosus
25 cm. A deep-bodied, laterally compressed little fish, with a relatively large head and small terminal mouth. Dorsal fin in two parts, the first with 10-11 strong, sharp spines, increasing in length so that the last is almost as long as the first branched ray to which it is joined; 10-12 branched rays. Anal fin continuous with 3 spines and 10-11 branched rays. Scales small, firmly attached; 35-47 in lateral line. Brightly coloured with blue lines across the head, speckled on the body; gill cover has a bold black spot at its edge with a narrow border of yellow and a small crescent-shaped red mark on the extreme edge.

Distribution: native to eastern North America; introduced in the early 1900s to Europe and now widespread north of the Pyrenees and Alps.

Natural history: in America lives in lakes and sheltered parts of lowland streams, preferring weedy areas. Forms schools and can be seen near the surface on clear sunny days. Feeds on insect larvae and crustaceans; adults consume some small fishes. Breeds May-June in shallow nests dug in sand and gravel patches between weed beds. Eggs hatch in 3-5 days; the young mature at 2-3 years and may live for 9 years.

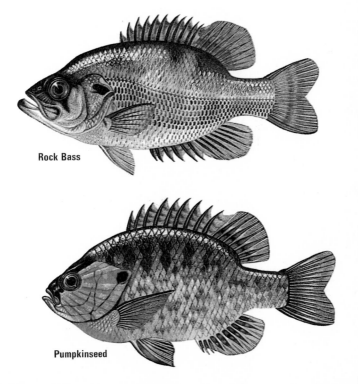

Rock Bass

Pumpkinseed

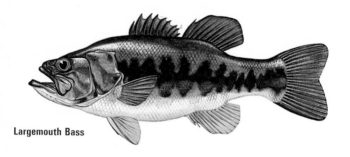

Largemouth Bass

LARGEMOUTH BASS
Micropterus salmoides
83 cm. A rather slim fish with a rounded body and large head. Mouth large and oblique, the upper jawbone extending well past the level of the rear of the eye. Dorsal fin continuous but deeply notched, with 9-10 strong, sharp spines and 12-13 branched rays. The dorsal fin spines are longest in the middle of the fin, becoming shorter where they join the branched rays. Anal fin with 3 strong, short spines joined to the 10-12 longer branched rays. Scales covering most of head and all of body, small, firmly attached; 60-68 in lateral line. Back dark olive-green, sides golden-green fading to white on belly; a solid black stripe with zig-zag edges runs from head to tail.

Distribution: originally found in North America in the Great Lakes and the Mississippi system; now widely distributed both in North America and Europe.

Natural history: lives near the surface of shallow lakes and in slow-flowing rivers; particularly abundant in areas where plant growth is dense. Young fish live in shallow water, large ones in deeper areas but rarely below 6 m. Breeds March-July in nests dug in sand and gravel. When young eats crustaceans and insect larvae, but as it grows feeds increasingly on fishes. A serious predator on native fishes when introduced into restricted waters.

SMALLMOUTH BASS
Micropterus dolomieui
68 cm. A rather slender but cylindrical body with a large head; mouth large and oblique. The bone forming the upper edge of the jaw reaches only to the level of the front of the pupil. Dorsal fin continuous, shallow dip between spiny and branched ray parts of the fin; spines short and strong, 9-10 in number; branched rays 13-15. Anal fin with 8 strong short spines and 10-12 branched rays. Scales well developed on most of head and entire body, small and firmly attached; 68-78 in lateral line. Pelvic fins joined together by a broad membrane at base, and by a smaller membrane to body. Faint dusty bars on sides.

Distribution: native to eastern central North America; widely redistributed in America, Europe and elsewhere. Occurs sporadically in western Europe.

Natural history: prefers to live in open water over rocks or sand in rivers and lakes; often found in rivers where the current is moderate but tends to shelter close to rocks or fallen trees. Breeds May-July in a nest made by male in sand or gravel; male guards the eggs, which hatch in 4-5 days, and the larvae. 5,000-14,000 eggs are laid per female. Feeds on aquatic insects and crustaceans when young; mainly on fishes when older.

Right: this North American species was introduced to Europe mainly for its angling potential.

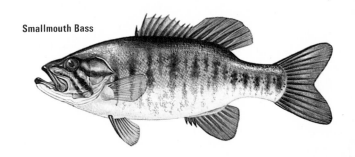

Smallmouth Bass

PERCH FAMILY
Percidae

The perch family are freshwater fishes which are widely distributed across the northern hemisphere. Members of the family occur naturally across northern North America, with the exception of Alaska and the Pacific coastal rivers, and from England eastwards across Europe and northern Asia. Because some of them are popular as anglers' fishes and in some cases are good to eat, they have been widely redistributed both within this range and outside it. Members of the family have been introduced to Ireland and, in the southern hemisphere, to Australia, New Zealand and South Africa.

All perches have two dorsal fins, either separate or narrowly joined at the base, the first comprised of slender spines. The anal fin has one, rarely two, spines and a series of branched rays. The pelvic fins have one spine and five branched rays and the fins are placed well forward, usually beneath the pectoral fins. The body is covered with rather small, firmly attached scales which have fine teeth on their free edge. These give the body a rough feel when handled. Scales also extend over much of the head and most members of the family have flattened spikes on the gill cover although they are not sharp enough to inflict any injury when the fish is handled. Most perches have large jaws with numerous rows of teeth; in many species, particularly the fish-eating ones, the teeth are enlarged into curved fangs in the front of the jaws. Small teeth are also present on the inside of the mouth and throat.

Three major evolutionary lines are recognized in the family which, according to some researchers, merit sub-family rank. These are the true perches (perch, ruffe and others) with a serrated margin on the anterior gill cover and a well-developed swimbladder; the darters (small fishes of North America) which have a smooth-edged anterior gill cover and either no swimbladder or a small one; and thirdly the group containing the zander and the zingel, which are slender-bodied and have a swimbladder (zander) or none at all (zingel).

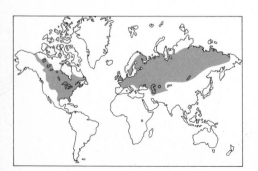

Right: the strong spines in the dorsal fin of this perch are typical of all the members of the family. There are about 126 species in this family of freshwater fishes, most of them are the small North American darters, Etheostoma sp. Some species, like the perch, have been introduced to the southern hemisphere.

Perch

PERCH
Perca fluviatilis
51 cm. Relatively deep-bodied with a short head, blunt snout and large mouth. Two dorsal fins, separate but very close together at their base. Dorsal fin with 13-16 slender spines; second dorsal with 1 spine and 13-16 rays. Boldly marked with dark bars on back and sides, bright red pelvic and anal fins.
Distribution: across Europe from Ireland (where introduced) to Siberia, except for much of Norway, Spain and Italy.

Natural history: typically a fish of pools, lakes and lowland rivers. Stays close to weed beds, well camouflaged by its coloration. Breeds in small schools April-May in shallow water, the female shedding eggs in a lacy mat over weed beds, twigs and occasionally the river bottom. The eggs hatch in about 8 days at 13°C. The young feed on planktonic crustaceans, then also on insect larvae and later small fishes. As large fish, perch tend to become solitary, and will dominate a water eating the fry of all fishes including their own. They may live for up to 10 years.

RUFFE

Gymnocephalus cernuus

30 cm. Body moderately deep but head large with a blunt, rounded snout and rather small mouth. Head scaleless with the skin covering large blister-like cavities on the cheeks. Dorsal fins continuous, the first with 11-16 slender spines, the second with 11-15 branched rays. Anal fin with 2 long spines and 5-6 branched rays.

Distribution: from eastern England across Europe and Asia to Siberia; absent in the Iberian, Italian and Balkan peninsulas.

Natural history: essentially a fish of lowland rivers and lakes, living near the bottom in small schools. Feeds mainly on bloodworms (the larvae of non-biting midges) which burrow in the mud, but will also eat other small insect larvae and crustaceans. Breeds March-May, the eggs sticking to stones and plants. They hatch in 8-12 days and the young mature at 2-3 years. Ruffe rarely live as long as 5 years.

Left: the ruffe lives close to the bed of slow-flowing rivers and feeds on midge larvae.

STRIPED RUFFE

Gymnocephalus schraetzer

30 cm. Slender-bodied with a long, large head. Similar to the ruffe but its snout is much longer, being approximately half the head length. Two dorsal fins joined together; the first fin with 17-19 long, slender spines, the second with 12-14 branched rays. Anal fin with 2 long, slender spines and 7 branched rays. Head scaleless but with large blister-like cavities under the skin on the cheeks.

Distribution: lives only in the River Danube from its middle reaches to the sea.

Natural history: little-known and apparently uncommon, the striped ruffe lives in deep water in slow-moving stretches of the river and its backwaters, usually close to a sandy bed. Feeds on bottom-living crustaceans, insect larvae and occasionally molluscs. The hollow cavities on the cheeks and lower side of the head are thought to play a sensory role, helping the fish find buried food. Spawns April-May, shedding the eggs over stones and plants in shallow water usually in a moderate current.

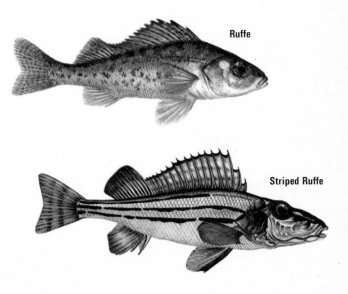

Ruffe

Striped Ruffe

ZANDER
Stizostedion lucioperca

1·3 m. Body elongate but cylindrical; head pointed. The upper jaw extends past the rear margin of the eye. Jaws large with several large curved fangs in front and numerous smaller teeth. Two dorsal fins; the first spiny with 13-17 sharp, slender spines, the second with 2 spines and 19-24 branched rays. Anal fin shorter than second dorsal with 2-3 spines and 11-13 branched rays. Small, rough-edged scales on gill covers and upper part of head, and all over the body; 80-95 in lateral line.

Distribution: native to eastern Europe from the Baltic to the Danube; introduced to the Rhine and now spread through western Germany and France. Also introduced to England.

Natural history: abundant in large lakes and lowland rivers, preferring cloudy water. Hunts most actively in the twilight, lying close to the bottom and keeping still at other times. When young it keeps in schools but older fish tend to be solitary. A top-level predator, as an adult it eats virtually any smaller fish, including its own young. Breeds April-June over stones or a sandy bottom and on the roots of water plants in shallow water. 13,000-125,000 eggs are laid per female.

ASPRETE
Romanichthys valsanicola

13 cm. A slender but round-bodied little fish with a broad head; blunt snout and small mouth. Two dorsal fins; separated by a short space; first dorsal with 9 spines, second with 15-16 branched rays. Anal fin with 1 spine and 17 branched rays.

Distribution: confined to a section of the River Argis, a tributary of the Danube in Romania.

Natural history: discovered in 1957 living in the upland river hiding under stones. Feeds on insect larvae. Though relatively common when it was discovered, changes in the river and in agricultural practices have caused the asprete to become very rare.

ASPER
Zingel asper

20 cm. A slender-bodied fish. round in cross-section but somewhat flattened

on the belly. The tail between the end of the dorsal fin and the tail fin is long and narrow. Two widely separated dorsal fins; the first with 9-10 slender spines, the second with 1-2 spines and 10-12 branched rays. Pelvic fins large and fan-like.

Distribution: found only in parts of the River Rhône system.

Natural history: lives on the river bed in rather shallow, fast-flowing water. Spawns March-April among stones in gravel, the eggs being buried between the stones. Feeds on bottom-living invertebrates. In general the biology of this species is very little known, and it is believed to have become rather rare.

STREBER
Zingel streber

20 cm. Body very slender, with the region between the second dorsal fin and the tail fin of pencil thickness. Two dorsal fins, well separated, the first with 8-9 slender spines, the second with 1-2 spines and 11-13 branched rays. Broad pelvic fins set far apart.

Distribution: found mainly in the River Danube and its tributaries; an alleged subspecies in eastern Greece.

Natural history: lives close to the river bed in small schools, usually isolated in colonies by its need for a habitat of sand or fine gravel bottom and fast-running water. Mainly active at night when it comes into the shallows to feed on bottom-living invertebrates. Spawns March-April.

ZINGEL
Zingel zingel

40 cm. Body long and slender, rounded in cross-section except that the belly is flattened. Tail between second dorsal fin and tail fin moderately long. Two well-separated dorsal fins, the first with 13-15 slender spines, the second with 1-2 spines and 16-18 branched rays.

Distribution: found only in the rivers Danube and Dniester and their tributaries.

Natural history: lives mostly on sand or gravel bottoms where the current is swift. Mainly active at night when it comes into shallow water to feed on bottom-living invertebrates. Breeds April-May on gravel banks, burying the eggs among stones. Now rare.

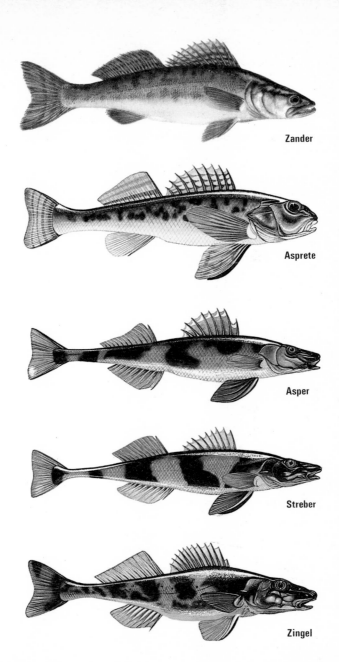

Zander

Asprete

Asper

Streber

Zingel

GREY MULLET FAMILY
Mugilidae

The grey mullet family is relatively large, containing about 100 species worldwide. They are mostly marine fishes, but many show an inclination to live in estuaries and brackish lagoons, while some tropical species live in fresh water most of their lives, returning to the sea only to breed. They are torpedo-shaped fishes with blunt, broad heads and medium-sized mouths, with no teeth in the jaws but fine teeth on the lips. Their two dorsal fins are widely separated; the first has four slender spines, the second one spine and several branched rays. The scales are large.

THIN-LIPPED GREY MULLET
Liza ramada

60 cm. Slender, streamlined body with a broad blunt head. Mouth wide, set at tip of head; thin upper lip (narrower than half the eye diameter); teeth on lip minute and bristle-like. The dorsal fins, well separated; the first with 4 sharp, slender spines. Pectoral fin short, if folded forwards does not reach the eye. Dusky spot at upper edge of pectoral fin base; anal fin dusky.

Distribution: from the southern Baltic, Norway and the British Isles south across the Mediterranean.

Natural history: a schooling fish which lives mainly in the sea but enters rivers and estuarine lagoons, in summer in northern Europe, and all year round in the Mediterranean. Feeds on mud scraped up with its lips, and on green filamentous algae browsed from rocks and harbour walls. Most of the mud eaten is indigestible. Breeds in the sea in late summer; young fish common in coastal waters in their first year.

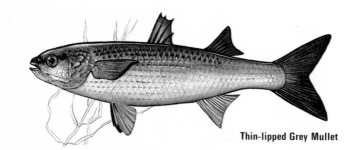

Thin-lipped Grey Mullet

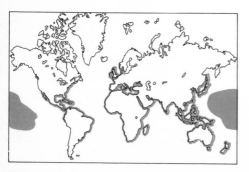

There may be about 100 species in this family of mainly coastal marine and estuarine fish, but there is much confusion over the exact number. Some live entirely in fresh water, as in the Caribbean islands.

BLENNY FAMILY
Blenniidae

There are about 275 known species in the blenny family; about 20 species are found in Europe, most in the Mediterranean, and only one of these lives in fresh water. They are slender, scaleless fishes with a blunt head. The dorsal fin is long and continuous, the first rays being slender, flexible spines, the remainder segmented; the anal fin is similar in shape but shorter. The pectoral fins are broad and fan-like. Blennies have a series of relatively large, closely-packed teeth in their jaws. They usually live in shallow coastal waters, often on the shore line.

FRESHWATER BLENNY
Blennius fluviatilis

15 cm. A rather stout-bodied fish with flattened sides. Head small; mouth small with numerous teeth in the jaws. Profile of head steep – mature males develop a fleshy crest along top of head. Small-branched skin flap above each eye. Body scaleless. Dorsal fin long; 12-14 simple, flexible spines, 15-20 segmented rays. Anal fin with 2 short flexible spines and 15-20 segmented rays. Pelvic fins beneath the rear of the head; each with 3 finger-like rays.

Distribution: the blenny lives in brackish lagoons, freshwater rivers and lakes all round the Mediterranean except for the arid African coast.

Natural history: the only blenny to be found in freshwater in Europe. Lives in slowly-flowing as well as still water, feeding on small crustaceans and molluscs. Breeds May-June, laying eggs under a stone which are guarded by the male. The eggs, stuck to the underside of the stone, are 1 mm in diameter; the young fish are 3 mm long at hatching.

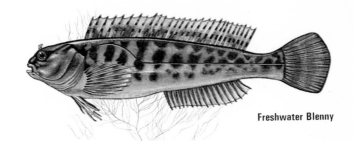

Freshwater Blenny

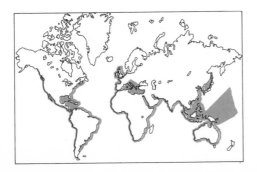

There are about 270 species in this family of small, mostly marine, fishes. A few are found in brackish and fresh waters, but they are most abundant in tropical and warm temperate seas in shallow water.

119

FLATFISH FAMILY
Pleuronectidae

Flatfishes are placed in a separate order of fishes (Pleuronectiformes) because of their distinct appearance and their unique development. On hatching from the egg, the larval flatfish looks similar to other fishes with an eye on each side of the head. During its late post-larval development, one eye moves across the top of the head to settle close to the other eye on the side of the head. Following this change, which involves complex twisting of the optic nerves and muscles, the whole of the head changes shape and the fish turns on its side and settles on the sea bed. There are several families of flatfishes, most of them marine fishes, and these have their eyes on the right or left sides according to their family placement. Only one flatfish, the flounder, is found in fresh water in Europe and this belongs to the family Pleuronectidae. These mostly have their eyes on the right side of the head, while the left side of the head and body are unpigmented. The flounder is often found 'reversed' – that is, its eyes are on the left side of the head, which is also dark coloured. Although found in the sea, it often migrates far upstream into fresh water.

Flounder

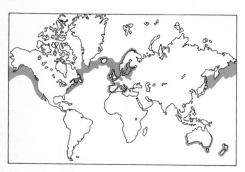

Most members of the family are marine fishes, usually living in shallow inshore waters. They include the plaice, dab and halibut, and several other important food fishes.

FLOUNDER

Platichthys flesus

51 cm. The only European freshwater flatfish. Eyes usually on the right side of the head (locally about one third of any one population may be 'reversed'). Bases of both dorsal and anal fins have small, sharp prickles, and there is a patch of prickles just above the pectoral fin. Anal fin rays 35-46; dorsal rays 52-67 – no fin rays spiny.

Distribution: coastal waters of Europe from the White Sea southwards to North Africa and the Mediterranean and Black Sea. Abundant in the freshwater Baltic Sea and all river mouths and many rivers.

Natural history: lives on the bottom in rivers using the tidal flow to move upstream, but in fresh water moving upstream in short bursts of activity. Spawns in the sea in spring; the eggs and early young are surface-living and move inshore and into estuaries at a length of 2-3 cm. Feeds on crustaceans in rivers; larger fish also eat molluscs. Also common in coastal waters as many flounders do not enter fresh water. In the sea it lives in inshore waters from the tide line down to 50 m. Close to the coast, it migrates up to the shore as the tide advances, feeding on worms, cockles and crustaceans which mostly lie hidden in the sand or mud during low tide and emerge to feed as the tide comes in. Is more active at night than by day. In keeping with its estuarine habitat, the flounder is most common on muddy bottoms but it is also frequently found on sand as well as stony bottoms. The tendency to migrate into fresh water seems to be more pronounced in cooler latitudes. In Scottish freshwater lochs near the sea the flounder is abundant, as it is throughout the Baltic Sea, but in the south of its range it is less common in purely freshwater habitats.

The only European flatfish to live in fresh water; it usually keeps to muddy estuaries, moving upstream with the tidal flow, but does occur up to 100 km from the sea.

GLOSSARY

adipose: in salmon family fishes, the small fatty fin in front of the tail which has no rays.

aestivate: resting during the summer's heat; opposite of hibernate.

barbel: fleshy sensory organ developed on the lips and round the mouth; used for locating food.

caudal peduncle: narrow part of the body just in front of the tail fin.

characin: member of the family Characidae; South American and African freshwater fishes.

contact organ: a white blister-like organ developed by male carp family members at spawning time.

cusp: one lobe of a tooth.

diatom: minute single-celled alga with a hard silaceous (sandy) shell.

encrusting algae: simple plants which grow underwater on stones or wood, often covering them in a green mat.

eutrophication: enrichment of the water, often by agricultural fertilizers, or sewage; also occurs naturally.

filament: a long, slender protrusion, as in a gill or an extended fin ray.

filamentous algae: simple plants which grow in long branching threads; looks like green cotton wool.

gill raker: the white cartilaginous projection on the inner side of the gill arch; used to retain food in the throat.

keel: sharply compressed and usually deep edge to the body.

migration: purposeful movement of animals in the same general direction.

nematode: a type of minute worm, common in the soil, on plants, in the river bed, and as parasites.

ostracod: small crustacean with two curved shells; most common near the bottom mud and on plants.

pectoral fins: the pair of fins behind the head; level with the eye in the perch family, lower down in most other fishes.

pelagic: living at the surface and drifting with the movement of the water.

phytoplankton: minute single-celled plants, living near the water's surface; basic food of zooplankton.

process: a pointed part of the skeleton, or an elongate scale.

protrusile: in fishes usually the jaws which are hinged so that they move forwards to select food items.

rotifer: wheel animalcules; microscopic animals which have a feeding and locomotory organ composed of long vibrating cilia which beat in sequence, and look like a wheel.

scute: an enlarged, hard, sharply-ridged scale on the body of a fish.

silt: fine bottom mud usually with a high organic content, inhabited by minute animals.

swimbladder: gas-filled bladder within the body cavity of a fish beneath the spine. Used to help the fish float, but also a sound transmitter.

tubercle: creamy white, horny growth on the skin, developed in spawning male carp family fishes.

vent: in fishes refers to the combined opening of the anus, urinary, and reproductive tracts.

zooplankton: small drifting animals near the surface; in fresh water mostly small crustaceans.

INDEX

ACKNOWLEDGEMENTS

The author and publishers wish to thank the following for their help in supplying photographs for this book on the pages indicated:

Heather Angel, pages 24, 27, 29, 31, 43, 55, 63, 79, 86, 93, 105. Bruce Coleman, pages 67 (Hans Reinhard), 97 (Hans Reinhard), 111 (Timothy o'Keefe). David Hosking, pages 76, 83, 114. Natural Science Photos, pages 51 (Don MacCaskill), 72 (L. E. Perkins). Nature Photographers, page 121 (C. S. Bisserot). A. Van den Niewenhuizen, pages 8, 61, 71, 113.

Maps by MLJ Cartographics

Picture Research Penny Warn